Label Launch

D0596130

Also by Veronika Kalmar

Start Your Own Zine: A Jet Lambert Gumption Guide

Label Launch

A Guide to Independent Record Recording, Promotion, and Distribution

Veronika Kalmar

St. Martin's Griffin ☙ New York

www.stmartins.com

Book design by Michael Collica

Library of Congress Cataloging-in-Publication Data

Kalmar, Veronika.
  Label launch: a guide to independent record recording,
  promotion, and distribution/Veronika Kalmar—1st ed.
    p. cm.
  Includes index (p. 187).
  ISBN 0-312-26350-3
    1. Sound recording industry—Vocational guidance.
  2. Alternative rock music—Vocational guidance. I. Title.

ML3790 .K264 2002
780'.68' 8—dc21   2001059871

10 9 8 7 6

This book is dedicated to my brother Erik,
who should rescue his wife's vinyl collection.

Contents

Acknowledgments

Thanks to the following people for their assistance and support in making this book a strong and thorough resource for all the delightful folks foolish enough to dedicate their lives and careers to indie music:

Carrie Akre
Julianne Anderson
Dawn Anderson
Glen Boyd
Mimi Crocker
Joe Ehrbar
Jack Endino
Scott Frampton
Craig Holzer
Marty Jourard
Myles Harlow Kahn
Tess. Lotta
Barbara Mitchell
Al Moss
Alicia Rose
Hayley Tapp
Dawn Tunnell

And an extra-special groovy thanks to Nabil Ayers and Vanessa Veselka for their support, knowledge, and endless patience.

Research Assistants & Reviewers

Robert Allen
Eva Dohertry Gremmert
Tess. Lotta
Myles Harlow Kahn
Heather Rogers

I first discovered indie labels when I stumbled across KCMU, a then–low-wattage punk rock station sponsored by the University of Washington. It wasn't long before I dyed my hair purple, started sucking on clove cigarettes, and began to frequent the sweaty firetraps that passed as clubs in pregrunge Seattle. It was utopia. Of course, this scenario had repeated itself an infinite number of times far before my birth. But my naiveté—and that of my friends—set us up for an adventure, one that we shotgunned along with the cheap, generic beer that kept us wobbling through days of record-store rummaging, nights of ratty rock 'n' roll, and early-morning after-hours parties and debauchery.

Eventually I scored my own radio show at KCMU, where I consumed a good dose of music history and opened my ears to a variety of genres I never knew existed. It did little to quell my punk rock snobbery, but I realized that all music has value. I listened to everything from punk to blues to world beat to reggae to industrial to techno. Search long enough and every genre offers an intriguing sound, space, emotion, or vibe, I discovered. Meanwhile, my pals were touring, booking bands, and fighting to write about an emerging sound in a city where no one seemed to care.

People worked, people got screwed, people made mistakes—but we were having fun, and listening to amazing music that blew our minds and drove us to share.

Unfortunately, innocence can't last forever. Grunge exploded and, in some ironic cases, became exactly what it had started out playfully mocking—bloated, overblown arena rock. Suddenly, some of us were making either a full or partial living from our hobby. We made mistakes, and often those mistakes hurt our friends and co-workers. Even worse, certain folks started treating music like it was a *business.* Seems they didn't want to pull lattes to support their auditory habit. The choice of how to balance the importance of releasing music with the reality of finances often proves a point of contention for independent labels. It breaks bands and the people who work to support them into two groups: those who brave the pursuit of music as a business and those who prefer to endure the monotony of most day jobs. Neither path is right or wrong. It's simply a choice.

I eventually accepted a position at a regional rock magazine called *The Rocket,* and after two and a half years, left to start my own rag, *The Iconoclast,* which concentrated on emerging music and the culture surrounding it. Starting a quarterly zine also allowed me to restore my indie cred, take a day job as a technical writer and enjoy creature comforts I had forgone since leaving my parents' home. During my two-and-a-half-year stints with each magazine, I saw new indies, the bands that they signed, and the people who supported the records released on those indies make the same mistakes my friends and I had made. Despite the fact that the music kept mutating, the indie business surrounding it essentially stayed the same. Hence this book.

Label Launch: A Guide to Independent Record Recording, Promotion, and Distribution is written to help new label owners and owners of growing indies avoid common traps and to educate all individuals involved in indie music on the various aspects of the biz. I wrote it wearing all four of my literary hats: technical writer, business writer, journalist, and rock critic, in that order. Both the business and the art of music prove technical, and my goal was to communicate often difficult and confusing information in an organized, clear, and concise manner.

Although I possess a strong knowledge of print, Web, and radio, and a general knowledge of most of the other aspects of indie music, the journalist in me interviewed experts in each field for several reasons, first, to provide authoritative information, second, to enlighten the reader to the point of view held by individuals in each profession, and third, to sate my own curiosity. There were simply things about some aspects of the indie music industry that I just wanted to know, and writing a book proved a good excuse to have people explain them to me. Finally, I wanted to avoid the embarrassment of having people doze off reading often dense content, so I channeled the critic to chat through chapters in a manner that did not disturb the actual information.

A successful indie can be anything from a label that puts out periodic singles to a serious endeavor that releases three or four records a year to a tightly run business that grooms bands for major labels. All require a different level of investment, and all prove equally legitimate. An indie CD can break even at about 1,200 copies. This assumes the band pays for recording and that you do all the promotion. The sale of 5,000 CDs is commonly considered indie gold. Few records reach that point, but the numbers don't matter. Indie labels exist to expose music that might not otherwise be heard, and there is no shame in losing a few smackers to further that cause. This book is designed to provide you with the information necessary to take you from your first release to regional distribution and national recognition. However far you choose to pursue that path, I thank you for your effort, dedication, and insanity, and I look forward to enjoying the records you create and support. Good luck.

Cheers,
Veronika

Veronika Kalmar
PMB 283
117 E. Louis St.
Seattle, WA 98106

1 A Brief History of Indies

Many music purists think of indie labels as a late 1970s phenomenon, but the history of renegade music mavens committing their most beloved bands to vinyl began far before London street punks started sporting Mohawks and dyeing their hair colors normally only found on the feathers of peacocks. Indie labels have been a viable part of the music industry for more than fifty years. Punks merely rediscovered a DIY (do-it-yourself) ethic and a system long used by other disenfranchised but wily entrepreneurs who launched indie labels so a limited number of fans had access to obscure or emerging music.

The cycle works like this: indies keep their ear to the street and discover new talent while major labels empty the veins of the last set of trends built by indies. Some trends hit it big, others exist just above the radar. In either case, majors generally dilute a new sound so it appeals to the broadest market possible. They're big businesses, that's their job. Eventually, the mainstream industry falls into a slump and the general public, hungry for a new sound or cultural vibe, catches on to something that has been rumbling underground and the next megatrend is born. Indie bands sign to majors and become stars, small labels develop distribution deals with, or are bought out by, big record companies and in five to ten years, the cycle begins again—usually with new indies and often with new genres. Certain genres, namely folk, jazz and, to a certain extent, rock, always boast a healthy "underground" scene. Though the major-buys-out-indie cycle repeats itself at least once every decade, most indie labels fail to make their owners rich in anything other than the ability to share their obsession of a specific genre with like-minded souls. In other words, running an indie label is not a career, it is a calling.

1947–1957:
R&B Meets Hillbilly Music

The first major wave of indies occurred in the 1950s and served artists of color and what was then known as hillbilly music. "Hillbilly" referred to Appalachian-tinged country derived from the folk music brought to the U.S. by Irish immigrants. As hillbilly music took root, black artists continued to develop different strains of jazz, blues, and R&B. Eventually, they reclaimed swing and morphed the sound into a high-energy genre christened jump-blues (which reemerged in the 1990s as the postmodern swing of bands like Big Bad Voodoo Daddy).

In the early 1950s, hillbilly and jump-blues collided to form a sound that caught the fancy of the world's first generation of teenagers. For the first time in history, young adults had extended their childhood into puberty. Rock 'n' roll proved not only a perfect aphrodisiac for late-night necking but also an excellent way to trip out all-American parents who freaked as their teenage daughters screamed in ecstasy every time they heard the sultry voice of a white, southern country boy named Elvis Presley.

Elvis and Sun Records brought rock 'n' roll to the mainstream. Owned by producer Sam Phillips, Sun Records grew out of a Memphis recording studio. The indie first gained attention by releasing rhythm and blues greats such as Rufus Thomas. After hitting the charts with five singles by Elvis Presley in 1954 and 1955, Phillips sold his star's contract to RCA and used the cash to develop future greats including Johnny Cash, Carl Perkins, Roy Orbison, Charlie Rich, and Jerry Lee Lewis.

While Elvis and Sun inevitably get most of the glory associated with the emergence of rock 'n' roll, numerous labels—the most notable of which were Atlantic, Atco, and Chess—contributed to the rise of the genre. Atlantic Records cut a path for rock 'n' roll indies by offering jazz and R&B artists a kind and welcome outlet. Formed in 1947 by Herb Abramson and Ahmet Ertgun, the label expanded its format in the 1950s and released records by Ray Charles, Ruth Brown, Joe Turner, the Clovers, and the Drifters. In 1955, Abramson formed a subsidiary, Atco, which developed a licensing agreement with the production and song-writing team of Jerry Leiber and Mike Stoller. The duo produced a string of hits for the Coasters including "Youngblood," Atco's first single to sell a million copies.

Another major contributor to the 1950s rock 'n' roll boom was Chess, a label formed in the first year of the decade by two brothers, Leonard and Phillip Chess. Using the Atlantic/Atco model to achieve crossover success, the Chicago-based label focused on urban blues with down-home grit by releasing the work of Muddy Waters and Howlin' Wolf. Although the brothers developed their most successful rock 'n' roll act, Chuck Berry, on Chess, they launched Checker, a label dedicated to country blues, in 1952. Checker carved out a unique niche built around the blues harmonica: first with Little Walter, harmonica player for Muddy Waters's backup band, and later with Sonny Boy Williamson. The label also released albums by Lowell Fulson, the Flamingos, and Bo Diddley, who eventually moved to Chess.

1958–1975:
The Golden Era of Indies

As the 1950s drew to a close, new indies emerged as a major force in the music industry; this despite the slow demise of Chess/Checker (purchased by GRT in 1972) and Sun, which ironically began to fail after Phillips upgraded his studio and consequently lost the unique acoustic sound that made his label famous. Between 1962 and 1966, independent record labels, as a group, scored more Top 10 hits than major labels. At the top of the heap stood Barry Gordy, who founded Motown in 1959.

Born in the Motor City, Motown holds the honor of providing the model for indie success: get an image, get a sound, and promote the hell out of both. While most indies of the 1950s had the first two, Gordy was the first to successfully market a label as not only a musical movement but as a lifestyle. Smooth, soulful, and stylish, Motown made savvy black chic safe for the masses. During the same time period, Vee Jay discovered the Beatles; Atlantic and Atco sugarcoated pop; Del-Fi hit the beach and Rounder infiltrated the U.S. via the post office.

Motown first achieved success in 1960 with the Miracles' "You Better Shop Around." A short year later, the Marvelettes hit number one with "Please Mr. Postman." Gordy, who kept a firm grip on his acts and vision, coached his performers on public appearances. With the songwriting team of Brian Holland, Lamont Dozier, and Edward Holland, he scored a string of hits by the Temptations, the Miracles, the Supremes, Marvin Gaye, Stevie Wonder, the Four Tops, Martha and the Vandellas, and the Isley Brothers. The label's reign lasted through the sixties, but seemed to falter after Holland/Dozier/Holland left in 1967 and Gordy moved the company to Los Angles in 1973. Barry sold the label to MCA in 1988.

If Motown provided a blueprint for indie success, Vee Jay demonstrated Murphy's Law in action. Despite the label's early accomplishment as an outlet for black music (John Lee Hooker, Jimmy Reed), the Chicago-based indie—launched in 1953 by Vivian Carter and James Bracken—ran into an array of troubles during the 1960s. Vee Jay first crossed over to the mainstream market in 1962 and 1963 when the Four Seasons scored three number-one hits. Carter and Bracken also obtained the rights to the early recordings of a then-unknown band called the Beatles from Capitol. Unfortunately, legal disputes would sour the label's relationship with both their crossover band and Capitol. Vee Jay ended up in court when they were charged with failure to pay royalties to the Four Seasons, and after the Beatles hit in 1964, Capitol rescinded the indie's licensing agreement.

Of all the early indies, Atlantic and Atco weathered the musical storms of the 1960s most successfully. Atlantic broke the Queen of Soul, Aretha Franklin, and expanded their roster to include rock and pop in the midsixties. In addition to the cheery sound of Sonny & Cher and the Ras-

record shop in 1976. Owner Geoff Travis specialized in punk records and set up a distribution network that eventually led to a label. Rough Trade released a wide variety of genres—agitpop, reggae, punk—and boasted artists from both sides of the Atlantic including the Go-Betweens, Aztec Camera, the Smiths, Stiff Little Fingers, the Fall, the Raincoats, the Dream Syndicate, Camper Van Beethoven, Everything But the Girl, and the Jesus and Mary Chain. The label flourished until it suffered defections and the Rough Trade distribution network faltered. However, the trimmed-down label still exists and continues to release new material.

Eventually, two California musicians, Jello Biafra of the Dead Kennedys and Brett Gurewitz of Bad Religion, launched U.S.-based labels that carried their own and other bands. Formed in June 1979 in San Francisco to release the Dead Kennedys' debut single "California Uber Alles," Alternative Tentacles, the U.S.'s first punk indie, quickly relocated to Europe but returned after Americans bought imports of the compilation album *Let Them Eat Jellybeans* in significant quantities. Biafra followed the compilation with singles from D.O.A., Flipper, and TSOL, plus albums by the Butthole Surfers, D.O.A., Nomeansno, and the Dicks, to name a few. The label also releases spoken word recordings and remains artist-driven, limiting releases to one-offs (no multiple-album deals) and giving bands full creative control.

Although it sprang from the same root, Epitaph tread a different path in terms of growth and philosophy. Formed in the early 1980s to release records by Bad Religion, the label signed other punk bands including Rancid and NOFX. Epitaph experienced such success that Gurewitz left Bad Religion in 1993 to dedicate himself fully to the label. One year later, the Offspring released *Smash,* which sold eight million copies. Both the Offspring and Bad Religion signed to majors and Epitaph expanded their roster to include an array of swing and ska-punk hybrids.

Punk was not the only genre to tap into the strength of indies. Both rap and art-rock took advantage of independent production, marketing, and distribution to introduce crews and artists either a bit too intellectual or a bit too avant-garde for the mainstream. Tommy Boy, a New York-based rap indie, and 4AD, a British-based label, sat at the top of their respective heaps.

While the majors flooded the market with rappers boasting of their endowment, Tommy Boy primarily released material focused on social, cultural, and political issues. Tom Silverman launched the label that pioneered the fusion of rap with European electronic music. In addition to introducing innovative acts such as Afrika Bambaataa, Tommy Boy broke through to the mainstream with Queen Latifah, Digital Underground, and De La Soul. The label took a decidedly more commercial bent in the 1990s with acts like Naughty by Nature and Irish-American rappers House of Pain. Their continued success led the label to sign a deal with Warner Bros. in 1994.

4AD has remained independent since its inception in 1980. Formed by Ivo Watts-Russell and Peter Kent, Watts-Russell continued to spearhead the label after Kent left to set up Situation 2. She did a phenomenal job by quickly developing a top-notch roster that included the talents of The The, the Birthday Party, Tones on Tail, and the Cocteau Twins. The Cocteau Twins set the tone and vision for the label. Their ethereal art-rock, and the distinctive sleeve designs by Vaughn Oliver's 23 Envelope studio, came to symbolize the label. Other major acts from this period include Colourbox and This Mortal Coil, Watts-Russell's own studio project. In the late 1980s, the label expanded their roster with Dead Can Dance, Wolfgang Press, Throwing Muses, and the Pixies, a band with a decidedly unique, but un-4AD sound. The Pixies gained not only critical acclaim, but also mass acceptance. As the label began its second decade, it continued to expand the genres it offered by releasing records by Lush, the Breeders, and Belly.

The most successful indie of the 1990s was Matador. Founded in 1991 by Chris Lombardi, the label rapidly expanded its roster when Lombardi joined forces with former Homestead owner Gerard Cosley, who had developed acts including Sonic Youth and Dinosaur Jr. Together the team signed numerous breaking artists, the most notable of which were Liz Phair, Bettie Serveert, Yo La Tengo, and Pavement. Their endeavors proved so successful Cosley left the States to open a European branch of the label in England and Matador linked itself first with Atlantic and later with Capitol Records. In 1999 they dissolved their major label ties and retained the rights to all their artists with the exception of Phair.

2 Sub Pop: A Model

Near the beginning, I remember Bruce Pavitt thinking of this explicitly: Charles Peterson would be the look; I was supposed to be the sound. They would create an identity and hype it. Motown was exactly the model Bruce and Jon had in mind.
　　　　　　　—Jack Endino, producer and innovator of the Seattle Sound

With its enormous success and relative longevity, Sub Pop colorfully depicts everything that can go right *and* wrong with a record label. Sub Pop has launched a musical revolution, endured extreme financial difficulties, and had periods of internal feuding; it also made its founder, Bruce Pavitt, and co-owner, Jon Poneman, millionaires. But before you decide to revel in the glory of indie fame and fortune, consider the following.

Sub Pop originated as a fanzine produced by a quirky Olympia, Washington, resident named Bruce Pavitt. After publishing *Subterranean Pop* for a year, Pavitt expanded his indie empire by releasing a collection of demos from unknown punk rock bands in 1980. Considering that U.S. music fans were just beginning to open their ears to the then-rebellious and decidedly noncommercial genre, one assumes Pavitt was more concerned with making tapes of his favorite bands accessible to a very small market than with international acclaim. He also released a series of tapes from unknown artists as well as a vinyl compilation, *Sub Pop 100* (1986), and *Dry as a Bone* (1987) by Green River, a band that contained future members of Pearl Jam and Mudhoney.

Like many notable entrepreneurs and artists in Seattle, both Pavitt and Poneman explored other outlets that supported indie music. At the time, it was not uncommon for a local scene to be run and supported by a handful of individuals who performed multiple functions. Pavitt spun discs at KAOS at Evergreen State College, an internationally acclaimed institution noted for its build-it-yourself curriculum and lack of formal grades, while Poneman hosted a local music show and acted as promotions director at KCMU, the then-University of Washington College station in Seattle. In 1983, Pavitt turned his fanzine into a column in *The Rocket* magazine while Poneman sought out small venues above restaurants and in basements in which to book obscure bands.

Despite the limited size of the Seattle scene in the early 1980s, Pavitt and Poneman didn't first meet until 1987. Within a year they had formed an alliance bent on breaking Seattle bands into the mainstream consciousness. The two primary elements needed for success had emerged organically: an international audience tired of the drivel pumped out by major record labels, and most important, a solid base of bands, all located in one place, with a common look and sound. It wasn't planned; grunge had evolved naturally and was bound to break. Pavitt and Poneman simply took advantage of an existing situation. Still the ride wasn't easy.

The duo applied the Motown model to Seattle. Engineer/producer Jack Endino provided the sound; the image came courtesy of the blurred photographic style of Charles Peterson and the secondhand stores where musicians picked up Levis and flannel shirts for a few bucks a pop.

Between 1988 and 1992, Sub Pop would bring international recognition to Seattle, almost go bankrupt, introduce the world to Nirvana, and lose the majority of the acts that brought the label recognition. The first release of the Sub Pop Pavitt/Poneman era was *Screaming Life* by Soundgarden. That same year, the band—which eventually transformed their sound from grunge to metal—would release an EP, *Fopp*, leave Sub Pop for SST, and eventually sign with A&M. Nineteen eighty-eight was also the year Sub Pop initiated several brilliant marketing moves that succeeded in creating an international buzz, but almost drove the label into bankruptcy. First, they flew British journalist Everett True, then a writer for *New Music Express,* to Seattle for a taste of bucolic grunge. They also hired their first employee, Daniel House, owner of his own indie, C/Z, to run a direct-to-retail distribution hub designed to service numerous indies, and launched their singles subscription club with "Love Buzz" by Nirvana. The well-planned rollout proved a success. True's articles made Sub Pop a sensation in England, which caused the rest of Europe as well as the States to take note. The singles club released monthly, limited-run, colored vinyl singles for a membership fee of $35, and later $40. Fans paid for their subscription upfront, which provided Sub Pop with interest-free investment capital. The combination of notoriety, talent, and hip-struck kids anxious to score limited run records fueled the label's rapid expansion that included offices in Boston, London, and Toronto by 1990.

Then came rumors of a Sub Pop demise. It became clear that the label's actual trade lagged behind its hype early in 1991. By indie standards, Sub Pop's sales proved phenomenal. Mudhoney's first full-length sold about 70,000 copies. At the time, most large indies needed to sell 5,000 copies of a disc to be considered gold. But the Sub Pop hype machine and shiny world-domination image boosted the break-even point of its records closer to that of a major label release. Sub Pop also neglected to sign formal agreements with the bands into which it poured significant promotional funds. Upon hearing the Seattle hype, major label A&R reps swooped down on the city luring away naive bands with fine-dining tours and large recording advances. Small, often underdeveloped bands wanted tens of thousands, rather than thousands, of dollars to ink a deal. In addition, Sub Pop lost or sold Nirvana to DGC, the Screaming Trees to Epic, and the Los Angeles–based all-female act L-7 to Warner Bros. Suddenly, singles club members started receiving their monthly vinyl ninety days late. Eventually, Sub Pop dissolved its distribution center, had its vinyl printed through a third party in Europe, and signed a pressing and distribution (P&D) deal with Caroline. The label that had started with less than $20,000, launched the careers of many of the world's soon-to-be-famous bands, and opened an array of international offices started hawking T-shirts that sported the phrase, "Which Part of 'We Have No Money' Don't You Understand?"

Luckily, Sub Pop did ink a contract with a small trio from Aberdeen,

Washington, named Nirvana. To acquire the still relatively unknown geniuses in 1991, DGC paid $72,000 and promised Sub Pop 2 percent of any future royalties the band earned. Bingo. An album named *Nevermind* and fourteen million copies later, Sub Pop found themselves suddenly solvent. But with most of the talent drained from Seattle, and the label's trademark sound diluted by major label imitators, Sub Pop groped for new acts. The label continued to sign bands with musical relevance—most notably Sunny Day Real Estate—but their new stable lacked the communal strength of a local scene and the cohesive sound that made Sub Pop famous. Fickle fans either outgrew their obsession with music or went in search of new sounds or the next big thing. In 1994, Pavitt resigned from the day-to-day operations of the label and in 1995, the dynamic duo that launched the legendary label sold 49 percent of their ownership to the Warner Music Group for a reported $20 million.

Since that time Sub Pop has experienced high- and low-points, much like any indie and business would. Nothing and no one is on top forever, especially in the music industry. Sub Pop does prove that the Motown model can still work on both a small and a larger level, and that even if a label makes numerous fumbling mistakes along the way, the right ears and learning by experience can lead to a successful indie.

3 Small Business Law

Stay away from a partnership if at all possible. Consider going for a lesser corporation. That way, you're not personally liable for the debt.
—Tess. Lotta, musician, booking agent, and international accountant

From the time you get your business license until well after you shut down shop, the legal aspects of the music industry will swirl about you in an almost opaque haze. Fear not, a good and communicative lawyer can help you maneuver the maze of jargon and almost limitless options. Keep in mind that laws and regulations differ from state to state, including basic organization matters. In this chapter you'll learn:

- The importance of a business attorney
- The benefits of various types of business registrations including:
  - corporations
  - limited liability companies
  - limited liability partnerships
  - limited partnerships
  - general partnerships
  - sole proprietorships
- The importance of trademarks

Although the content of this chapter is well researched, it is important that you review all legal information with an attorney to ensure your rights are protected. The following is not written by a lawyer or an accountant and does not qualify as professional advice. It simply provides a layman's overview.

Business Registration

Sometimes the type of business registration your indie needs is clear, and in other instances, you must weigh the pros and cons of the various forms offered in your state. A single indie can morph registration types over the course of its existence as well. You may start as a sole proprietorship because of the simplicity, change to a limited partnership when you get an investor, and become a limited liability company when you need more protection. Before launching into the humdrum of business registration, here are some terms you need to know.

Accounts payable: what you owe other people or businesses

Accounts receivable: what other people or businesses owe you

Amortization: the way start up expenses, investments, and intangible assets (assets you cannot touch, such as trademarks, patents, copyrights, and franchises) are expensed and subsequently deducted from taxes over a series of years

Assets: tangible and intangible properties such as cash, inventory, and the label name

Capital gains: when the price received for the sale of a tangible asset (a.k.a. plant assets) is higher than the price you paid for it

Depreciation: the way tangible investments (investments you can touch, such as buildings) are allocated or expensed as a cost of doing business and subsequently deducted from taxes over a series of years as the asset loses value. The deduction that you take annually for the capital assets over the time of their allocated lives as you use them in business

Expenses: Costs related to your business that are tax deductions

Liability: being held legally responsible for something; also investments that do not turn a profit and money owed to other people. Also an obligation on the balance sheet

Limited partner: an individual who contributes funds to a label
and does not take part in the day-to-day operations

General partner: an individual who contributes funds to a label
and takes part in the day-to-day operations

Payroll taxes: the amount of an employee's federal and state withholding, social security, and Medicare as well as federal and
state unemployment and income tax that an employer must
withhold and pay to the government

Perpetual existence: a label that exists after the owner or one of
the owners dies or leaves

Retainer: a method of paying a lawyer in advance by placing funds
in an account from which the attorney draws on a monthly
basis

Sole proprietor: the sole owner of a label

Finding a Business Attorney

Like it or not, it's important to work with an attorney when starting an
indie. And if your label grows, you'll more than likely work with a number of lawyers with various specialties. If you are lucky, you will find one
attorney who can help you set up your business *and* take care of the
basics of copyright law. Chapter 4: Music Law provides details on what
to look for in a music attorney. For now, we'll concentrate on how to
score and pay a lawyer that fits your business needs.

As with most things, the best way to find an attorney is through word
of mouth. Potential folks to ask include bands or other fools in the music
industry and small business owners. It would of course be ideal to find
someone who has worked with other indies. If you cannot collect recommendations, contact your local chapters of Volunteer Lawyers for the
Arts, then the local bar association to see if they have a referral program.
Once you have your list of potentials, it's time to conduct interviews.

Find out if the individual has done the type of work you need. At a minimum, you'll require someone with experience in setting up small businesses, preferably for artists and ideally for small indie labels. At this point, you also need to determine if you want this lawyer to help you with music law, in which case he needs extensive knowledge in, and experience with, trademark, service mark, copyright, and entertainment law. Then there is the ever-lovable issue of money. . . .

Lawyers are expensive. That's a given. And their billing systems prove complicated. After you select a lawyer, he or she will probably want to be paid in advance, in the form of a retainer, which is fine, as long as you know what you're paying for. A retainer is an advance payment that is placed in a bank account and drawn from as the lawyer performs the work. An attorney can also charge against the retainer for things like copies made and travel conducted on your behalf. Due to these often hidden costs, it is important to determine up front exactly what you want and how much you will be charged for it, including items like copies. By the way, attorneys start at about $175 and you need to include a phrase in your fee agreement that indicates you have a right to opt out of the relationship at any time. You and the lawyer can then agree on how long your initial retainer will last and continue with the relationship thereafter if you both wish. Finally, a lawyer should be able to give you a ballpark figure for a specific job based on his hourly billing and the number of hours he expects to spend performing a task. In some instances, you can negotiate a flat fee or a cap for a particular job, such as drawing up articles of incorporation.

Business Registrations

I would advise against people putting in sweat equity. If you bring sweat equity into a partnership, make sure you know how much you make an hour in the beginning. If you have no prior agreement to the value of your sweat equity, you can't claim that as an asset for your partner to buy out should you divide later.

—Tess. Lotta

Oh the glory of determining how to organize your indie. If this daunts you beyond belief, remember that there is more to come. Owning an indie means more than just releasing records, it means running a small business. Your primary options for business registration include:

- a corporation
- a limited liability company (LLC)
- a limited liability partnership (LLP)
- a limited partnership
- a general partnership
- a sole proprietorship

Most indie mavens will discover that registering their label as an S corporation, a limited liability company, or a sole proprietorship best fits their needs. Truth is, the optimum registration for you depends on the size of your company, the number of people involved in the venture, and the value of your personal assets, like homes, cars, and record collections containing rare and valuable vinyl and CDs. Unless the state you live in restricts you from starting a limited liability company, there is really no reason to run an indie as a corporation. One can start a limited liability company individually in most states or as part of a partnership in all states. That said, it is important to work with someone knowledgeable of the type of protection a limited liability company in your state receives. Often, a limited liability company offers almost all the same benefits as an S corporation, however, there are exceptions.

Running your label as a corporation or limited liability company offers the most protection for your personal property. Anyone with a lot to lose, like a house and investments, should consider a limited liability company. Limited liability partnerships offer some of the protections of a limited liability company, while general partnerships lack those protections and divides ownership of all assets (tangible and intangible properties such as cash, inventory, and the label name) equally unless otherwise legally arranged. Finally, sole proprietorships operate simply and require only a business license, an EIN number (available from the IRS), and a few extra forms (usually a Schedule C) at tax time. You need to acquire an EIN from the IRS if you are planning to have employees.

Corporations

Corporations are complicated. You'll need a lawyer, an accountant and a hefty amount of personal assets to start one. While corporations limit personal liability and provide an array of deductions, they are complicated to set up and maintain. What sets a corporation apart from a partnership is that it is its own entity. Rather than being owned by an individual or set of partners, the entity issues stock, which allows people to purchase a piece of the company. Because a corporation is its own entity, you—the primary shareholder—generally will not be held liable for the actions of the company. During litigation closely held corporations can be pierced and the individual shareholders held responsible. In order to qualify for this indemnity, you'll need to file articles of incorporation and deal with corporate tax law. It is best to retain at least 51 percent of the stock in your company, as Sub Pop did when it sold a large chunk of itself to Warner Bros. It is the only way to truly retain control of your business.

The actual act of incorporating a business is expensive so expect to set aside a minimum of $2,000 for issuing stock, reserving a name, and paying filing fees. Once you have worked through this maze, you can become buddies with your accountant, who will help you understand corporate tax structure and its deductions, which include deductions for employee benefits. One of the interesting aspects of running a corporation is that you end up working for the corporation and potentially even collecting a paycheck. This means you'll have to send yourself W-2 forms and fill out a personal 1040 form at tax time. Your corporation will also pay social security, state and federal unemployment, and income taxes. The good thing is that, if your corporation goes belly up, you may be able to collect unemployment, providing you were getting paid. Further details on taxes are provided in Chapter 5: Setting Up Shop.

If you own an indie and choose to incorporate, you will most likely choose to become an S corporation because this form allows shareholders to report their portion of the corporation's taxable income on their personal tax return. S corporations must file a form 2553, "Election by a Small Business Corporation," with the IRS during the first two-and-a-half months of your company's tax year. In addition, an S corporation must file form 1120S, "U.S. Income Tax Return for an S Corporation," by March 15 and present shareholders with a copy of Schedule K-1, "Shareholders Share of Income, Credits, Deductions." Finally, there are many restrictions to starting an S corporation. The ones you will primarily be concerned with are the requirements that you must incorporate in the United States, you may not have a nonresident foreigner as a shareholder, and you cannot have more than seventy-five shareholders.

Limited Liability Companies

Limited liability companies offer the ease of operation of partnership or an individual proprietorship and, depending on the state, a form of limited liability similar to that of a corporation. Anyone launching a label should closely examine this option and the numerous benefits it has to offer. One can start a limited liability company individually in most states or as part of a partnership in all states.

The primary benefit of a limited liability company is that, given the right situation, it can provide significant tax benefits for sole proprietors and general partners. In addition, this form often limits individual liability for all partners and sole proprietors. In other words this form can, *in some instances,* protect your personal investments (like a house or car) if your company goes bankrupt or someone sues your company.

The tax benefit derived from running a limited liability company for partners and sole proprietor is the ability to deduct losses from your personal income because you are self-employed. It is important to remember that while daily operating expenses are deductible on an annual basis, the cost of equipment—like computers or recording equipment—will be depreciated over a series of years as the equipment loses value.

Limited liability proves another important benefit of limited liability companies. In general partnerships and, depending on the state, limited partnerships, a general partner is partially liable for not only business debts and legal claims but potentially for their partner's personal finances as well. These business forms allow creditors and individuals who file other claims (such as copyright violation) to peruse the personal assets of the owners. In addition, if one of your partners files for personal bankruptcy, his creditors can file a claim against the partnership, but not you personally.

Limited Liability Partnerships

Although you should definitely consider a limited liability partnership if you are going into business with one or more partners, this beastie is barely out of the birth canal and therefore vague in the areas of both taxes and what type of liability is limited. Limited liability partnerships offer the ease of operation of a general partnership with significant pro-tection for individuals involved in the venture. In general, limited liabil-ity partnerships protect one partner from the illegal actions of the other(s). Since laws vary greatly from state to state, it is important to work with a lawyer or accountant to set up your business and determine what type of protection is offered in your state. In addition, a professional can inform you of the necessary forms you need to file—often annually—to initiate and maintain your status as a limited liability partnership.

Congress is still debating how to handle taxes levied on limited liabil-ity income, so work with an accountant when setting up your business and doing your taxes. In addition to the tax confusion, you may or may not be personally liable for other things such as the following, depending what state you live in:

- Litigation regarding your partners bad decisions, for example, copyright violation
- Debts to creditors if your company goes bankrupt

If you opt to start a limited liability company, you are always liable for your own poor decisions. Finally, if one of your partners declares personal bankruptcy, her creditors might be able to tap the partnership for retribution.

Limited Partnerships

If you've heard of silent partners, then you understand the concept of limited partnerships. One or more people provide the brains and talent, while one or more separate individuals fork over the capital. In other words, limited partnerships have both general (active) partners and limited (silent) partners. Each type of partner has very different legal responsibilities. Limited partnerships were created to allow individuals not involved with the day-to-day operations of a business to invest in a partnership without having to accept personal liability for the business's finances and actions. This person would be the limited partner. General partners, on the other hand, are pretty much liable and responsible for everything. Each state has different requirements regarding limited partnerships, so it's best to contact an attorney familiar with the legal requirements in your area. You'll need to have a lawyer draw up articles of organization to start the company anyway.

For the general partner, limited partnerships can provide significant tax benefits but no protection from personal liability or the effect of your other general partner's poor personal finances on the business. The tax benefits derived from running a general partnership can include deducting losses from your personal income, select limitations on moving money from your business accounts, and no unemployment tax. Unless you have employees, most limited partnerships do not need to pay special federal income taxes, although the owners do need to file form 1065 with the IRS. They receive a K-1 from the partnership with income and expenses. They then fill out a Schedule E in addition to their 1040 tax form and pay taxes as a self-employed individual. This allows general partners to deduct loses from their business against the taxes they pay from earnings on their day jobs. It is important to remember that daily operating expenses are deductible on an annual basis, but the cost of equipment—like computers or recording equipment—will be depreciated (expensed and deducted over a series of years as the equipment loses value).

There is one extremely important aspect for every general partner to consider before entering a limited partnership. This type of agreement makes you partially liable for not only business debts and legal claims but also potentially for the other general partners' personal finances as well. In a limited partnership, creditors and individuals who file other claims (such as copyright violation) can pursue the personal assets of the general partners. In addition, if one of your partners files for personal bankruptcy, his creditors can file a claim against the limited partnership.

For the limited partner, things are much simpler. She can only lose the money she invests in the company. Period. They are not responsible for errors of judgment made by general partners, plus they don't have to pay self-employment tax. Yippee! One word of caution, there are limitations on loss deductions if the business shows a loss at the end of the year.

General Partnerships

If you are releasing records with a partner who is actively involved in the business and with almost no possibility of legal or financial complications, you might want to consider a general partnership, although if you qualify for a limited liability company, the latter would probably prove a better option. The primary benefit of a general partnership is that, given the right situation, it can provide significant tax benefits. The primary drawback to a general partnership is that it offers no protection from personal liability and your partner's poor personal finances can affect the business. While you do not need a legal agreement to start a partnership, investing in a lawyer to create a partnership agreement up front could save you from spending bundles in attorney fees if the partners start having disagreements and the partnership splits up.

The tax benefits derived from running a general partnership can include deducting losses from your personal income, select limitations on moving money from your business accounts, and no unemployment tax. While most general partnerships do not need to pay special federal income tax, the owners do need to file form 1065 with the IRS. They receive a K-1 from the partnership with income and expenses. They then fill out a Schedule E in addition to their 1040 tax form and pay taxes as a self-employed individual.

This allows individual owners to deduct their business losses against the taxes they pay from earnings on their day jobs. Remember that although daily operating expenses are deductible on an annual basis, the cost of equipment—like computers or recording equipment—will be depreciated. Another benefit of self-employed status is that the owners generally do not pay unemployment and payroll taxes unless they have employees. The ease with which individual owners can move and withdraw business funds depends on how you set up your formal partnership. For the most part, the tax implications of moving funds prove minimal. It is important, however, to consult an accountant who can fill you in on the pros and cons of your choices.

One aspect to consider before entering a general partnership is that the agreement makes you partially liable for not only business debts and legal claims, but potentially for your partner's personal finances. In a general partnership, creditors and individuals who file other claims (such as copyright violation) can pursue the personal assets of the owners. In addition, if one of your partners files for personal bankruptcy, her creditors can file a claim against the partnership.

Although you are not legally bound to file papers when starting a general partnership, it is wise to work with a lawyer. General partnerships are rarely, if ever, a fifty-fifty proposition and defining terms up front by allocating income, expenses, equipment, and losses can greatly reduce headaches and heartaches when you and your best buddy have disagreements or part ways. It could save you money in the long run. Make sure to determine:

- Who will provide which assets? Determine value of sweat equity in writing.
- Who will perform what amount and kind of work for what compensation?
- How will profits be split and taken?

Another item to keep in mind is that partnerships are not perpetual—which means they cease to exist if one partner leaves or dies—unless the owners indicate the business is to continue after one or more partners leave in a legal agreement.

If one or more of the individuals entering a partnership already own a business, it is highly recommended that you not rely on the existing registration but get a new one. That way everyone's name will be on the paperwork. For example, your potential business partner already owns a record store and he or she wants to fold the new label into his or her master business license to circumvent the cost and hassle. Problem is, you are nowhere on the paperwork, plus the holder of the master business license can combine the books for the label and the record store. The result? You possess little legal claim to business losses (which could be a positive or negative thing) or the assets and equity of the label if it takes off.

Sole Proprietorships

If you are releasing records without a partner and with almost no possibility of legal complications, a sole proprietorship is for you. It is by far the simplest of all the business registration options. Plus, if given the right situation, a sole proprietorship can provide significant tax benefits, although you cannot deduct employee benefits such as life insurance. Other common benefits such as health insurance and retirement can still be deducted personally, just not against the business. Of course, if your company is that big and successful, you will probably run it as something other than a sole proprietorship for numerous other reasons. The primary drawback to a sole proprietorship is that it offers no protection from personal liability.

The tax benefits derived from running a sole proprietorship can include deducting losses from your personal income, almost no limitations on moving money from your business accounts, and no unemployment tax. Since you report your label's profits and losses by supplementing your 1040 tax form with a Schedule C, you can deduct losses from your business against the taxes you pay from earnings on your day job. It is important to remember that daily operating expenses are fully deductible on an annual basis, but the cost of equipment—like computers or recording equipment—will be depreciated.

When it comes to moving money around, sole proprietorships also prove to be the most simple form of business. First, you do not need to get permission from co-owners to withdraw funds from an account or to sell your assets because there are no partners. Second, since you are not employed by the business as you would be in the case of a corporation, you do need to pay self-employment tax on your personal return.

Finally, a sole proprietorship is the only form of business registration that does not require fancy legal papers to launch. You just decide to start a sole proprietorship, get the appropriate city, county, and state license, and bingo, you're in business. It is important not to be lured by the simplicity of this legal form of business if you have personal assets because it could cost you your home or record collection.

Trademark

Trademarks protect business names. Before you select a name, make sure it does not infringe on someone elses. Several methods exist for conducting searches for currently trademarked names. You can perform an informal search using the Net, carry out a formal search using a lawyer or a private trademark researching firm such as Thomson & Thomson, or search the U.S. trademark library via the Micropatent Web site (see Appendix for contact information). You can also reserve a name for up to four years by filling out an "Intent of Use" form. To turn the "Intent of Use" form into a trademark application, simply send proof that you have used the name in interstate commerce such as advertising in out-of-state newspapers or shipping receipts to out-of-town record stores. If you fail to use your trademark for two years, you legally abandon your rights to the name. On the other hand, if you've used the name continually for five years, you can file an "Affidavit of Incontestability," which prevents others in the same line of business from claiming the right to the name.

You can also register your trademark in your state only, but why bother? Similarly, U.S. trademarks are good in the States only. You must apply—preferably with the help of a lawyer—in each country in which you plan to do business individually. You can get more information about trademarks by requesting the booklet *General Information About Trademarks* from the Superintendent of Documents, Government Printing Office, Washington, D.C. 20402. Most trademark forms are available at the U.S. Trademark Office website or you can request the forms by mail (see Appendix).

4 Music Law

*We've never paid for a recording, we've never given an advance.
Every single deal we do is net profit. Once it breaks even, it's a
fifty-fifty split, which is becoming more and more common. A lot
of bigger labels are doing stuff like that.*
>   —Nabil Ayers, musician and co-owner of
>   Collective Fruit Records and Sonic Boom record store

Music attorneys are a breed unto themselves. They do everything from filling out trademark applications to negotiating huge deals with the majors. In fact, if a band wants to sign with a major, the first step will often be to hook up with a lawyer who has relations with a record company. Often, that lawyer will represent both the band and the major label. Of course, until you release one of your bands to a major label, you won't need that particular type of music attorney. You will, however, probably need one or more attorneys to help you tackle some of the details covered in this chapter, which include:

- the different types of music attorneys
- the ins and outs of copyright law:
  - sound recording rights
  - performance rights
  - compulsory mechanical licenses
  - copyright infringement
- the details of publishing:
  - basics of royalties

- ○ performance rights organizations
- ○ overseas licensing
- potential tenets of a record contract

Although the content of this chapter is well researched, it is important that you review all legal information with an attorney to ensure your rights are protected. The following is not written by a lawyer and does not qualify as legal advice. It simply provides a layman's overview.

Music Attorneys

You may need one attorney to help you with the legal aspects of your label, or you may need many. At a minimum you will need to establish a relationship with a lawyer who is knowledgeable about copyright and trademark law. If you enter into any types of formal agreements with your bands, you need someone to draft and negotiate the contracts. And plan to shell out more bucks if you sell your back catalog or release a band to a major label. Finally, should you end up in court, that will require yet another type of lawyer. Ideally, you'll find at least a couple of these types of lawyers wrapped into one handy person. But chances are the person who helps you set up your copyrights will not be the individual negotiating the release of a band to the big boys. It's generally a different set of skills and experience.

Start with a music attorney who will help you draft your contracts and take care of copyright and trademark issues. Keep in mind that even at this level it is best to have someone with experience in music law. So, during your initial interview ask your attorney who he or she has represented and what he or she has done for them. If you do decide to release a band to a major, it's time to find someone with a lot of experience. Many bands get peeved when a label actually negotiates their release. But if an indie invests time, talent, and money in developing a band, they deserve to be compensated for their efforts. In order to get that compensation, hire a lawyer who has experience negotiating with major labels. Most of these lawyers live in New York or Los Angeles and the best way to find one is by talking to folks you know that work with them. In other words, you'll probably need an introductory referral unless you have a particularly hot band on your hands.

Although it may be tempting to score the most prestigious lawyer in your area when you start your label, it's not necessarily the best path. Hiring the attorney who represents your local rock star heroes won't benefit you if he takes you on to help line his pockets but considers your label too small to take seriously.

Copyright

Copyright law prevents people from stealing songs and making unauthorized copies of records. A properly filed copyright protects both the performance rights and the sound recording of a song. In general, the composer and the publishing company retain the rights to the composition while the label owns the sound recording rights if they pay for the recording of the CD. The owners of a label can also run a publishing company and work directly with licensing organizations such as ASCAP and BMI to collect and distribute royalties. As if that weren't complicated enough, label owners and employees also need a working knowledge of compulsory mechanical licenses and copyright infringement. You can request these forms from the Copyright Office (see Appendix).

Sound Recording Rights

Label owners are primarily concerned with the copyright of sound recordings, which one acquires by filling out the SR form and notes by placing the ℗ symbol on the outside of a CD insert. When you copyright a sound recording, it helps prevent others from reproducing part or all of the record either as a sample or as a pirated product. Registering your sound recording rights also protects the lyrics and music of the individual songs on the CD. If you are merely licensing a recording from a band, they will probably retain the sound recording rights. The cost of processing for an SR form is $30 through June 30, 2002. You can request an SR form by writing the Copyright Office for Publications Section LM-

455 (see Appendix). Forms are also available on the Copyright Office website.

Performance Rights

Performance rights are noted by the © on the outside of the CD insert, but make sure your artists fill out a performance rights (form PA) application long before a record is pressed. This form, available through the Copyright Office, includes the following details to help authenticate the copyright of a song:

- Title of the work: The name of the song, or preferably a title for a group of songs to save on registration costs.
- Previous or alternative titles: Either the old name of a song—if it has been renamed—or any other titles by which a song may be known. For example, if fans call a song titled "The Long Winding Walk Home from Tipperary" the "The Long Walk," you would indicate the abbreviated name on the form.
- Nature of the work: The type of work being registered, in most cases music and lyrics.
- Nature of the authorship: The writer's name and nationality or residence, their birth date and, if necessary, the date of their death, whether the work was contributed anonymously or pseudonymously (under a fake or performance name), and whether or not it was "work for hire." You would check this box by the name of a person that he or she was hired specifically to write songs. By the way, it's vitally important that the hired individual has agreed in writing in the form of an acknowledgment or waiver. The "nature of the authorship," means what an individual contributed. For example, one band member may have written the lyrics and another the music.
- Year in which creation of this work was completed: The year someone finished a song. So if they started on December 31, 2005 and completed on January 1, 2006, the correct year would be 2006.
- Copyright claimants: This would be either the songwriter(s) or their

publishing company, if the group has transferred the rights of their songs to that entity (see publishing rights later in this chapter).

- Transfer: If copyright claimant is different than the writers, then you need to explain how the rights were transferred in this space.
- Previous registrations: A songwriter notes if they have previously registered a song.
- Derivative work or compilation: In other words, a band has to fess up to the fact that they borrowed something—even from themselves. An artist identifies that she put new lyrics to a traditional Irish folk song or wrote new lyrics to an old song she registered three years ago.
- Deposit account: Folks who register a lot of songs can open an account with the Copyright Office. They deposit cash in the account and the copyright office deducts from it when they register a song. If the songwriter has such an account, they can have a deduction made from the account by listing the name of the account holder and the account number.
- Certification: The person filling out the form must identify themselves as an author, other copyright claimant, owner of exclusive rights, or authorized agent of the person they represent, for example, a songwriter.

Even though the author of a song automatically holds the rights to a tune once it is fixed in tangible form (read: written down or recorded), they need to send in the form before a significant number of people hear it. Since one pays the same registration fee for either one song or a set of songs given the same title, many artists record several songs on a demo and register the entire tape. If they choose the later option they also need to fill out the CA form. After they have completed this form, an artist needs to send it along with a copy of their material (songs in the form of a tape or written notes and lyrics) and the appropriate fee ($30 through June 30, 2002) to the Copyright Office. You can request a PA form and CA form from the Copyright Office at the address and website noted in the Appendix.

Performance rights prohibit other people from publicly playing an artist's work—either live or recorded—without paying to use it. In other words, when ABBA reunite, they can't record or perform one of your artist's songs without paying for it. Performance rights also cover radio airplay as well as instances when a song is played in hotels, stores, restaurant, on TV, in a film, or in any other public situation. Finally, when a label releases a record, they generally agree to pay the publishing company a set amount for every record sold on a quarterly basis.

Compulsory Mechanical Licenses

The person who writes a song automatically retains the right to record it before anyone else. This is referred to as the "right of first publication" and the composer can either retain that right, sometimes preventing a song from ever being released, or they can sell it. After a songwriter records a number, anyone can cover the tune if they request a compulsory mechanical license, pay the accompanying fee to the copyright holder, and pay royalties to the songwriter and publisher. If someone wishes to record a song but cannot locate the owner, she can file a notice of intent with the copyright office stating they made a concerted effort to locate the copyright owner and failed. Permission to cover a song is usually attained through the Harry Fox Agency, a company that collects mechanical royalties and pays them to the folks who own the song. They also negotiate deals with records labels who wish to release cover versions of songs. You can contact the Harry Fox Agency, Inc./National Music Publishers' Association (see Appendix).

Copyright Infringement

Even though you don't plan to explore any incredibly unethical aspects of the business like piracy, you still need to know what constitutes copyright infringement—especially if any of your artists sample other records. In order to prove copyright infringement, the copyright owner must demonstrate two things. First, that the works are substantially similar, and second, that the person performing and releasing the record had access to the original recording or material. With regard to sampling, your artist obviously had access, and although sampling, scratching, and mixing are definitely an art form in their own right, you need to get clearance from the owner of the work being borrowed from to protect yourself. There is an age-old rock 'n' roll myth that you can lift three chords legally. This is *not* true! If you release a record that used the riff from a song for a main groove and it becomes well known, expect a call from an attorney. For example, the Verve sampled a riff from a Thousand Strings' cover of the Rolling Stones' "The Last Time" in the song "Bittersweet Symphony" and later found they had to give credit.

If your artist claims she has gotten clearance, include that fact in the contract and as proof to protect yourself and your label from liability. You may still be considered liable, or at the very minimum, be required to recall the records if a lawsuit comes up. You, or the band, can hire a sample clearance company to negotiate a clearance. Commonly used sample clearance companies include Clearance 13'8", Diamond Time Ltd., DMG, Inc., Sample Clearance Ltd., Signature Sound, Inc., and Songwriter Service (see Appendix).

Publishing

> *Publishing is a musician's pension plan. If an artist writes a song that gets spun a lot, it is the only thing she will continue to get a check from.*
> —*Vanessa Veselka, musician and owner of Yeah, It's Rock records*

Publishing proves a major source of income in the music industry. Despite the fact that he proves a poor performer, a good songwriter can make a healthy living by having other people record and perform his work. The owners of some indies also run a separate publishing company that retains part of the publishing rights to their artists' songs. The publishing company then licenses the song to an organization that monitors airplay of the tunes and, when necessary, goes after individuals who don't pay the required fees. Primary licensing organizations include ASCAP and BMI.

Publishing is confusing. Traditionally, publishing rights are split into two halves, the songwriter's half and the publisher's half. That may sound simple, but it's not. Why? Because there are numerous types of publishing agreements. In most cases, however, the songwriter gets *half* of the publishing income in addition to *all* of the songwriting income. This is commonly referred to as "copublishing." So, in reality the songwriter gets three-fourths of the income pie while the publisher gets one-fourth of the income pie. Yes, it *is* more than fair. The person wrote the song after all. You are giving up one-quarter of the right to your pie to have the privilege of getting any of the income at all. But like record contracts, publishing deals come in a variety of forms, including:

- Copublishing agreements: This is a standard agreement for bands that regularly release records. In this type of an agreement, the seventy-five-twenty-five royalty split is common. If you run a publishing company as an aside to your label, this is probably the type of deal you'll cut.
- Term exclusive songwriters agreement: In this type of an agreement, the publisher keeps all the publishing income for all the songs a person writes within a specific period of time. In exchange, they give the songwriter an advance on the writer's share of the income. These deals typically last for a year with the publishing company retaining an option to extend the contract for two to four years.
- Administration agreement: In this type of deal, a songwriter gives the publishing company a specific percentage of the publishing income to handle the collection and distribution of their total (songwriting and publishing) income.
- Single song agreements: These are usually used for a song that a publishing company hopes to sell to film or TV. In this type of an agreement, the publisher generally retains all of the publishing income.

From your end, there are three other publishing-related items to consider: fame, international royalties, and the band's general welfare. If one of your bands moves onto a larger label and you have the luck of selling the publishing rights to their songs, remember to keep at least a small piece for yourself in case the band becomes immensely successful. In addition, all publishing contracts should contain a clause about international royalties since overseas rates are significantly lower than those in the U.S.

Now we come to the band's welfare. Unless a group is very unorganized, they will probably start their own publishing company. In all fairness, if you want someone's publishing rights, you need to provide them with a hefty advance and the ability to effectively promote their songs.

Royalties

Why would anyone want publishing rights? So they can collect royalties, of course. Royalties are the way a song earns money and they come in three forms: mechanical, performance, and synchronization. In other words, each time a song is recorded and manufactured or played, the little bugger earns cash. Mechanical royalties are paid by a record label for the right to manufacture a product containing the song. If your publishing company owns the rights to a song your record label releases, your label has to pay mechanical rights to your publishing company. If another label releases the song, your publishing company collects the mechanical royalties from them. In cases where a band starts their own publishing company, your label pays mechanical royalties to the band. Performance royalties are collected by performance rights organizations like ASCAP or BMI. Synchronous royalties are paid when a song is played in a film or on TV.

Performance Rights Organizations

Performance rights organizations monitor airplay and live performances of a song and collect a fee for each time the song is broadcast or performed. They also collect synchronization royalties when a song is used in a film or on a TV show. Many folks assume these organizations monitor all stations 24/7; those people are mistaken. Performance organizations take a survey of select stations and then calculate how much each song receives based on that survey. The amount a song receives is determined by the number of stations that play the song during the survey time, the audience size, advertising revenue, and wattage of these stations. If a song is played on a television show, the amount collected depends on the number of stations that air the program on which the song is performed and the range and audience of those stations. So the Rembrandts, who recorded the theme song for the TV show *Friends,* make money for every first run and rerun of the series. For most indies, BMI proves the preferable performance rights organization since it monitors college and public radio stations which are more apt to play indie records.

Performance rights organizations distribute funds to both writers and publishers, so when someone fills out the clearance forms required to register a song with an agency, she must indicate who gets what amount of the writer's share of the publishing and who gets the publisher's share. The organization you select will send you clearance forms along with a contract when you request an application. Both ASCAP and BMI have regional offices. Their addresses and contact information are in the Appendix.

Overseas Licensing

Since international distribution proves a major pain in the fanny, many labels and bands prefer to license their product overseas instead. If you only retain the U.S. licensing rights to, rather than the ownership of, a CD, the owner of the master recording takes care of and receives the income for all overseas licensing.

If an indie owns the actual recording, it can license a record to an overseas label, which purchases the right to produce and sell your product outside the U.S. or in a specific region of the world. If a record seems highly marketable in a particular country or region, you can expect an advance, which you must repay from your royalties. If you just want exposure for your bands and your label overseas, simply ask for royalties. Whatever the agreement, make sure your logo appears alongside that of the overseas label. It's a great way to establish an international presence and will boost your clout in the States.

Record Contracts

> *It's crucial to have a contract. If something happens, you need to be set. When the money starts flowing in, things can get really complicated, so I'm a big proponent of being tidy.*
> —Carrie Akre, diva and part-owner of Good Ink Records

There is no such thing as a standard recording contract. They can range from simple licensing deals to complex agreements involving huge advances and cross-collateralization. At a minimum, a label usually presses and distributes a release. In these instances, the band retains the rights to the master recording, which they deliver to you along with the completed artwork for the CD. Regardless of how informal the deal, it's important that both parties are clear on who is going to handle which elements of promotion. Logically, the label needs to work to get a record into stores, but radio promotions, publicity, and advertising need to be addressed separately. Otherwise, either half of the party can wind up thinking the other half is not fulfilling their part of the bargain. There is little use in putting out a record unless someone takes on the responsibility of letting people know it exits. You need to decide:

- Where and when advertising will be placed
- Who will pitch the record to print and on-line media
- Who will work radio
- Who will do (and pay for) the mailings

While the aforementioned method is a pretty good description of how most indies start out, a recording contract can contain numerous additional elements, the most supposedly tempting of which is an advance. Advances are simply a loan made to the band on their future royalties. In its most basic form, an advance pays for the recording, but it can also be used to purchase new equipment, to cover living expenses, for promotions, for tour support, or for anything else deemed necessary for the success of the record. Advances are also usually attached to multirecord deals. At this point, a label is making a serious investment in an artist or band, which is inevitably accompanied by a somewhat complicated contract. Common elements of larger contracts include:

- Master copy ownership: Generally, whoever pays for recording a record retains the rights to the master copy. If a completed recording is delivered to you, the band retains the rights. If a label pays for the recording, it retains the rights.
- Points: Points are music-industry speak for the percentage a band receives for each record sold. The percentage usually hovers someplace between 9 to 13 percent for indies. A producer's points are usually taken out of the artist's points. This section also needs to detail whether the points are based on the retail or the wholesale price of a record.
- Legal awareness: This clause states that you advised the band to seek legal representation.
- Copyright clearance: This section indicates that the band has obtained clearance for all copyrighted work. This includes sampling other people's records.
- Custodial considerations for artists under eighteen: In many states, the courts must approve any contract signed by a minor to make sure it is in the child's best interest and to protect kids from stage parents.
- Technical satisfaction: This ominous clause gives the label the right to refuse a record because it is technically unsatisfactory or, more likely, not commercially viable.
- Delivery or Output Requirement: The band agrees to produce a certain number of records with a specific amount of time between each delivery.
- Options: The label has the right to extend a contract for a specific period of time after the release of each CD. For example, you sign

a band in January, they release a record in June, and you have until the February of the next year to decide whether or not to release their next album. This agreement is one-sided. In other words, the band oddly has no option. Of course, at this level, you're the person assuming the financial risks.

- Cross-collateralization: This helps a label recoup the investment they make when developing a band. For example, if it costs $10,000 to create and promote a band's first CD, and the revenues for the first record are $5,000, you can apply that loss to the revenues grossed by the group's second record.

- Exclusivity to the label: This clause usually allows people to perform on side projects but prevents them from releasing records on other labels for a specific amount of time.

- Advance expenses, a.k.a. all-ins: This section details recoupable expenses, in other words what the label plans to give the band and what the group has to pay for out of their royalties, which is pretty much everything. An advance or all-in is nothing more than a loan on royalties. It can include equipment, video production, recording expenses, living expenses, tour support, equipment, indie promoters or publicists, and just about anything else you can imagine.

5 Setting Up Shop and Developing Artists

I come at it with the idea that I'm going to lose every cent. An average release for me is $5,000. The question I ask is, "Do I like this band or like the record enough to lose $5,000 that I have to earn waiting tables?"

—Vanessa Veselka

You put out a record by your favorite band and instant recognition and fortune are yours. Dream on. Behind any glamorous facade lies extensive planning and grunt work. The same holds doubly true for serious underground success. In this chapter we will examine:

- Artist and Repertoire
- Trademarks, Licenses, and Logos
- Professional Assistance
- Taxes
- Employees

While keeping books and filing taxes seem mundane, all are requirements for a successful business, and indie labels are businesses— whether you plan to make money or not. But we'll start with the glamour, the artists, the music, the muse that lures you into this insane venture. We'll start with A&R.

Artist and Repertoire

We look for someone we know, we look for someone we like, and something we think we can sell.

—Nabil Ayers

A&R stands for "artist and repertoire," basically musicians and the music they perform. In the first half of the twentieth century, songwriters created tunes and musicians performed them. That started changing in the 1940s, and today a musician's ability to craft a song proves almost more important than his ability to perform it. When you consider talent, you obviously want a band with at least one member who can do both. That's the easy part. Where talent abounds, temperament often fails. The toughest part of A&R is building a relationship of trust with the artist while still running a label in a pragmatic fashion. So before you release a record, ask yourself if it is marketable.

Who Is the Audience?

You know that strange art-rock band who totally turns your crank, but has no other known fans? You probably don't want to release their record. While signing the right band requires a good ear, it also demands restraint and a gut for trends. The most brilliant of artists can flop if their music lacks an existing audience. If an indie label owner releases an excellent trash-rock record while the world's listening to techno, he fails not only the band, but also himself. Recording a CD is stressful, and so is having a flop. Music is circular. Wait until the band's time comes. That way both you and the band have a chance at success.

If the sound and time prove right, make sure the band possesses a following. It could be in clubs, on a local radio station, or at large basement parties. A buzz can start anywhere, but it needs to exist before you dump a lot of money into supporting or even lending your label name to a band. If 50 percent of what you put out sucks, folks won't risk buying an unknown entity on your label.

Can the Band Support the Record?

Don't even think of releasing a record unless you know the band both can and plans to work their butt off to support it. In most cases, this requires local gigging and often regional or national touring. Does the act play clubs on a regular basis? Do the members have jobs or other responsibilities that prevent touring? Will they do in-store performances or appear on radio programs to support the release? If not, why release a record they are not willing or able to promote?

How Stable Is the Band?

Stability, or lack thereof, comes in many forms. The ideal band contains a practical businessperson and a charming promoter. Actually more of these exist than you might think, and if you choose to work with a group that lacks one of the above elements, you—or the band's manager—will have to provide the missing ingredient in order to make the record a success.

Does the Band Have Prior Commitments?

Before you release a record, make sure that neither the band nor its individual members have unfulfilled record or publishing contracts. Many times people walk away from a commitment without realizing that it continues to legally bind them.

Remember to Clarify Expectations

The only thing louder than the music of many rock bands is the roar of their complaints. Artists frequently grouse that their record flopped due to poor label support; therefore, it's important to clarify exactly what type of backing an artist can expect and that the cost of that backing will come out of their royalties. Do this in writing. At a minimum, a band deserves good distribution, but any tour support, advertising, publicity, recording, and even pressing details need to be addressed (see Chapter Four: Music Law) before you record or release a record.

Trademarks, Licenses, and Logos

In order to run a business, you'll need to trademark your company name, apply for an employee identification number (EIN), request federal tax deposit coupons with your corporate tax number printed on them from the IRS, and spend a day downtown picking up the following: a state business license, a local business license (if necessary), a county business license (once again, if necessary), and a reseller's license. A trademark helps prevent anyone from launching a label using the name of your company. They can, however, use it for another type of business. For example, you can trademark "Tabletop" as the name of an independent label and someone else can trademark it as the name of a pizza joint. You can also reserve a name for up to four years by filling out an "Intent of Use" form. For more information see trademark discussion in Chapter 3.

It's also important to make sure your bands service mark their names. A service mark is similar to a trademark. While trademarks protect things such as compact discs, service marks protect services, such as live shows.

Otherwise, you may dump several grand into releasing a record by a group only to receive a nasty letter from another label's lawyer. If the band already has a following you can always modify the name. For example, in the mid-1980s there were bands named the Charlatans and the Charlatans UK.

You can obtain a federal employer identification number (EIN) from your friends at the IRS by filling out an SS-4 form if you have employees, or if you are running a corporation, limited liability company, or partnership. Although this may seem like mere annoying paperwork, you will find it hard to conduct business legally until you obtain one of these numbers. It is necessary for opening a bank account that lets you cash checks in your business's name and obtaining federal tax deposit coupons. Federal tax deposit coupons come in a booklet from the IRS with your corporate tax number printed on them. The IRS gleefully prints these with a number of boxes you can check to identify what type of federal tax you are paying (payroll, unemployment, or corporate income).

Finally, a reseller's license will save you thousands of dollars throughout the years. It frees you from paying taxes on anything that you plan to distribute for resale to the public, for example CDs and T-shirts.

Professional Assistance

> *A bookkeeper can help you to assess and make business decisions from a monetary point of view. This is especially helpful when you make key growth decisions.*
>
> —*Tess. Lotta*

In order to run a business, you'll need to select a lawyer, an accountant, and unless you can remove yourself emotionally from figures, a bookkeeper. You'll also need to create a business plan and identity for your label, trademark your company name and logo, and acquire the required business licenses.

Lawyers

In the major label world, lawyers cut the deals. They often negotiate mind-boggling advances and get acts signed to major labels. Their role in the indie world proves a bit different. The level of experience you need in a lawyer varies depending on your planned activities. At a minimum, the lawyer you select needs a strong understanding of intellectual property rights. Once you start dealing with options and cross collateralization, you need a lawyer well versed in music law.

It is important to work with an attorney when starting any kind of business. And if your label grows, chances are you will work with a number of lawyers with various specialties. If you are lucky, you will find an attorney who can help you set up your business and take care of the basics of copyright law. As with most things, the best way to find an attorney is through word of mouth. Potential folks to ask would include bands or other folks in the music industry or small business owners. It would of course be ideal to find someone who has worked with other indies. Additional details on what to look for in a music attorney are included in Chapter 4: Music Law.

Accountants, Bookkeeping, and Taxes

The accounting and bookkeeping for an indie are complicated. For the basics, you can request a small business start-up kit from the IRS. Unfortunately, to meet all the legal requirements you may need two bank accounts and possibly someone to track international taxes and calculate royalty statements. In addition to keeping you legal, employing financial professionals will more than likely save cash in the long run since tax laws change annually.

To prepare your taxes at the end of the year, an accountant requires well-organized evidence of your income and expenses. A bookkeeper can set up ledgers to help you track these items. You can either have them create a system and log the information yourself, or hand over all your receipts and let an expert do the work. I recommend the latter. When the other aspects of running a label boggle your mind, a bookkeeper can provide clear direction and sound advice when it comes to finance.

Once you start to distribute internationally, a bookkeeper can help you avoid double taxation and recoup your costs. First they can chase down and track the withholding taxes that distributors pay in each country, then they provide your accountant with the information necessary to complete a double taxation form in the United States. In some cases foreign taxes can be deducted as a business expense. A savvy bookkeeper can help you identify these instances.

Bookkeepers can also eliminate common royalty disputes. Not only can they prevent the label owner from laboriously telling bands financial details they often don't want to hear, they act as a disinterested, number-crunching third party and help eliminate often unwarranted suspicions of book juggling. If a band questions their royalty statement, a bookkeeper can patiently, and without bias, explain what recoupable costs—promotions, cross-collateralization, etc.—were deducted up front and why. Biannual royalty periods generally end June 30 and December 31;

however, actual payment dates vary depending on contractual agreements.

Finally, label owners who also act as publishers must operate two separate businesses: a label and a publishing company. You'll have to have an account for each. To open those accounts you need a business license with a d.b.a. (doing business as). This allows you to legally conduct transactions under your business name. Don't give in to the temptation of combining your personal and business accounts. It will prove a nightmare if you are ever audited.

Taxes

> *It would be wise to understand payroll taxes. It's not difficult but there are timelines. If you don't pay them on time. You can be fined heavily.*
>
> —*Tess. Lotta*

The most important thing to know about business taxes is that they do not run on the same schedule as personal taxes. Plus there are a lot more forms to fill out. At the very least, the owner(s) of an indie will have to fill out their individual taxes (1040 form), plus self-employment (Schedule C) or partnership forms (Schedule E), or corporate taxes. They will also probably complete forms for employees, freelancers, or contractors. Since tax laws change frequently, it is important to work with an accountant to determine how to properly file your taxes

Personal and Corporate Income Tax

If your label is a sole proprietorship or partnership, you will probably file a few extra forms with your 1040. Sound simple? It's not, because you also have to make advanced payments of estimated federal and state income tax. In other words, the government wants their cash up-front. But only once you start to turn a profit, so most new indies will have a reprieve. A good bookkeeper is a goddess when it comes to quarterly taxes. On the federal level, all those involved in groovy, profit-making indies must shell out their estimated taxes quarterly using form 1040 ES. Installments are due April 15, June 15, September 15, and January 15. For example, for your 2002 taxes, you make your first installment in April 2002 and the last one in January 2003. Any leftover taxes are due on April 15, 2003.

Contractor and Employee Taxes

Making quarterly payment on your personal income tax is way easier than maneuvering the maze of corporate income tax. They also require you to shell out quarterly payments, but in this case you need to put the funds into an authorized government depository bank. Taxes are computed on a 1120-W form, which you can pick up at any IRS office. You'll also undoubtedly end up filling out forms that pertain to either independent contractors—a.k.a. freelancers or musicians—or employees. Forms for payments made to contractors are simple. You file a 1099-Misc for each contractor to whom you have shelled out more than $600 and to each musician whom you have favored with $10 or more in royalties (sounds a bit skewed against artists, doesn't it?). In order to fill out these forms properly, you need an individual's social security or EIN number. Make sure to get them up front, otherwise you must withhold 31 percent of their payments to make sure the IRS gets their share. This proves a bookkeeping nightmare and generally gathers a freelancer's undies in a bunch. Send a copy of an individual's 1099-Misc form to them by January 31. The IRS also requires you to summarize all of a label's 1099 information on a 1096 form and mail it, along with your 1099-Miscs, to the IRS by February 28.

Taxes for employees prove a bit more complicated than those for contractors. For starters, an indie must pay at least a portion of them. You'll need to fill out paperwork for income, social security, and unemployment tax. In addition, you will probably also have to deal with worker's compensation insurance. Paying federal payroll, unemployment, and corporate income tax requires federal tax deposit coupons, which come in a booklet from the IRS with your corporate tax number printed on them. For the most up-to-date employer tax information, you can request

Circular E: Employer's Tax Guide from the IRS. If your indie grows and you can afford it, consider hiring a company that specializes in processing payroll taxes. A payroll company makes all the required deposits and then sends reports to your bookkeeper.

Your commitment to employee taxes begins the day you hire someone, courtesy of the W-2 form. Anyone who has worked legally in the U.S. is familiar with this form. It's the one you fill out on your first day of work, or often, when you apply for a job. In addition to collecting vital information such as an employee's social security number, it also determines the number of exemptions an employee claims and thus the amount of income tax you need to pay and withhold from her paycheck. You don't need to file these forms with the IRS unless an employee claims more than ten deductions.

To pay an employee's income and social security tax, you combine the amount you have collected for each tax and pay it to the IRS at one time. Indies with a significant number of employees must deposit taxes into a federally approved commercial bank or a federal reserve bank using a federal tax deposit form and a federal tax coupon (see explanation under the Trademarks, Licenses, and Logos section, this chapter) on a monthly basis. If you pay less than $1,000 in combined income and social security taxes, you may qualify to use form 941 and deposit the funds quarterly. In addition to paying half of an employee's social security taxes, an employer must withhold the other half of the taxes from an employee's earnings.

At the end of each year, you must send employees a W-2 form that states her taxable income and the amount of taxes paid by January 31. In addition, the IRS requires you to summarize all of a label's W-2 information on a W-3 form and mail it, along with your W-2s, to the IRS by February 28.

While you get to split payroll and social security taxes with your employees, an indie owner is responsible for all federal and state unemployment taxes. Any indie that pays more than $1,500 in wages to employees annually or has one or more employees for twenty consecutive weeks during a year must shell out a few extra bucks for federal unemployment tax (FUTA). To make unemployment tax deposits into a federally authorized bank, use the dreaded federal tax deposit coupon, this time accompanied by form 8109. Finally, if you have employees, you will have to pay your state's workmen's compensation, which is included as part of payroll taxes in some states.

Employees

Taxes are only the start of a complex maze of federal regulations that apply to indies with employees. Indies with employees also need to be aware of:

- Minimum wage and overtime
- Immigration laws
- OSHA (Occupational Safety and Health Administration)
- Workers' compensation
- Family and medical leave
- Discrimination laws
- COBRA
- ERISA (Employment Retirement Income Security Act of 1974)

A company's responsibilities to the government compliance fall into three categories: those required of all companies, those required of companies of a certain size, and those required of companies that offer their employees extra benefits.

Required of All Indies

All small businesses must obey minimum wage and immigration laws, meet OSHA requirements, and carry workmen's compensation insurance, which is included as part of the payroll taxes in some states. Many of these laws, particularly those relating to minimum wage and discrimination are basic human decency, but it's good to know the exact regulations in any case.

Minimum wage and overtime are governed by the Federal Fair Labor Standards Act (FLSA). There are two minimum wages, the first for adults, and the second for those under twenty for the first ninety days of employ-ment. Since minimum wages change, it is important to keep up to date on current minimums, although the requirement that you put up a poster supplied by the United States Department of Labor should take care of that detail. Overtime compensation is more complex. Most employees must be paid overtime if they work more than forty hours in a one-week period. Some employees—for example programmers, executives, out-side sales, and professionals—are excluded from overtime laws.

Before you ever employ an individual, it is important to complete a I-9 form, designed to prevent illegal aliens from working in the United States. The employee fills out the top part of this form and indicates whether he or she is a United States citizen, an alien (foreign national, not E.T.) with permanent resident status, or an alien with work authoriza-tion. If an individual does not fall into one of these three categories, they cannot legally work in the United States. You as the employer must verify an individual's ability to work in the United States by examining and making copies of a variety of papers that legally assure an individual's status. The types of documents viable for each individual are listed on the back of the I-9 form. Both you and the employee need to sign the form, and you must keep it on file and updated for the eventuality of a Immigration and Naturalization Service (INS) or Department of Labor audit or verification request. You can get I-9 forms and an instruction book from your local branch of the INS.

OSHA requirements vary drastically depending on what types of activities take place at your company. Therefore, it is important to work with an attorney with OSHA knowledge. At a minimum, an indie must post an OSHA notice that is visible to all employees and keep a log of industrial illnesses and injuries. This can range from reporting carpal tun-nel problems to back strain caused from lifting a heavy box of CDs. (See Appendix for OSHA contact information.)

Although not federally mandated, most states require businesses to carry workers' compensation insurance. This type of policy provides insurance for accidents that happen at work or illnesses that are related to work. Since you can be penalized for not having it, indies should start shopping for a policy or see if their state provides the insurance as part of employee payroll taxes long before they hire their first employee.

Required of Indies of a Certain Size

With the exception of the Equal Pay Act of 1963—which requires equal pay for men and women performing similar work—indies with fewer than fifteen employees are exempt from antidiscrimination laws. In addition, indies with fewer than fifty employees are excused from the requirements set out by the Family and Medical Leave Act of 1993. So, if you have more than fifteen employees here is what you can't do. (Of course, if you're a descent human being, you wouldn't do them anyway.)

- Discriminate against pregnant women and new mothers (Pregnancy Discrimination Act)
- Discriminate against people based on their race, religion, national origin, or disability (Civil Rights Act of 1964, Americans with Disability Act)

Required of Indies that Offer Benefits

If you offer employees benefits such as health insurance, profit sharing, etc., it is important to be aware of ERISA and COBRA laws. ERISA deals with fairness in fringe benefits and is complicated; you'll probably need to work with an attorney with experience in this area to make sure you are in compliance with ERISA regulations. COBRA guarantees that employees may continue on as a member of a group health insurance plan after they voluntarily or involuntarily leave the company. The indie, however, is not required to continue paying their premiums.

6 Business Plans and Financing

*When you start your business, you're going to have to do it with
personal finances. There are people called angel investors, who
look at indie businesses that have been going for a while and are
steady and secure. These people might invest in your company as
silent partners or stockholders. You can find a lot of these people
by networking with other small businesses.*

—Tess. Lotta

One of the least enchanting aspects of starting an indie is developing a
business plan and analyzing funding options. Creating a business
plan in your head is not good enough, you need to conduct the excruci-
ating and often way too sobering exercise of putting potential reality on
paper. The depth of your business plan can vary. Those who want to
release a single and distribute locally need only pull together a couple of
pages, while individuals bent on national distribution need a detailed
analysis of markets, distribution options, and promotions. If you plan to
obtain outside funding, you must include detailed financial statements in
your plan. This chapter contains:

- Elements of a business plan
- Sample business plan
- Financing information

Business Plans

A business plan allows you to pace growth and to plan fiscally around how you want to grow. Your basic business plan is the foundation. You should always have a business plan. It focuses your fiscal budgeting.

—*Tess. Lotta*

A business plans serves three major purposes: it draws a roadmap for you to follow, it provides an introduction of your company to those you plan to work with such as lawyers, publicists, and artists, and, if you look for outside investors, it provides them with the information they need to make an informed decision. You can get help in developing a business plan by contacting the Small Business Association, taking classes on entrepreneurship at local community colleges, buying software that helps you develop a business plan, or simply getting a book that outlines the various elements of the beast. Here we will briefly review some potential elements that can be included in a business plan and a sample plan for a start-up indie.

Elements of a Business Plan

Not every business plan requires all the elements listed below. Evaluate your situation. Are you a start-up? Are you an established indie looking for funding? Are you looking for national distribution? Each of these situations reflects an indie in a different stage of growth and therefore each circumstance requires a different type of business plan. Here are some of the elements a business plan can include:

1. Table of contents
2. Executive summary that briefly summarizes the entire business plan
3. Business overview
   - A mission statement that outlines what you will sell to whom

- A business structure, for example, a corporation, limited partnership, or sole proprietorship
- A description of your label and the audience it serves including the details of your local scene and an analysis of your short- and long-term audiences
- The context in which your label operates, for example, what is the current state of the local, regional, and national music industry and how you fit into it
- Current or proposed contractual agreements

4. Marketing Strategies
   - Your primary and extended geographic markets
   - A list of media that might play or cover your artists and their geographic location
   - An advertising plan and budget
   - A promotions plan and budget that would include publicity and promotional events or gimmicks
   - A competitive analysis that identifies similar labels and differentiates the music you release from their product
   - A description of your long- and short-term audience that includes:
     - Why will they buy your records
     - Their demographics and psychographics, either formally researched or gleaned from knowledge of the "scene"
     - Where and how they buy records
     - Where they go to see shows
     - What else they do in their spare time
   - A description of the type of image your label wants to present and how you plan to achieve that image

5. Operating procedures such as:
   - Recording
   - Pressing
   - Artwork
   - Distribution
   - Marketing and promotions

- Marketing research
- Physical space requirements
- Inventory and supplies

6. Personnel
    - A detailed description of owner experience, both in business in general and in the music industry in particular
    - A list of additional resources including who will play which roles in the company (A&R, production coordinator, marketing, etc.)
    - An analysis of what outside resources you plan to utilize for promotions, legal assistance, accounting, bookkeeping, etc.

Note: Investors want to know that you, or members of your staff or consulting team, have experience in planning, organizing skills, controlling, and leadership.

7. Financial Data
    - A general statement of how much you have to invest and the amount of return you desire
    - A start-up budget that details equipment needs, license and permit costs, supply costs, legal and professional fees
    - An operating budget that details facilities needs, pressing and promotions costs, projected supply expenses, utilities, legal, professional and royalty fees, as well as depreciation and projected income
    - A set of current and projected financials. This is especially important if you want to attract investors. Financials determine how much cash you need, project your expenses, estimate your revenue, and set your sales and profit goals. They generally include a preliminary balance sheet, a list of assets (what you own) and liabilities (what you owe), and your operating and start-up or capital budget.
    - An implementation schedule that identifies how much money you will need and when

8. Appendix, where you include band bios, press clippings, print out of promotional Web pages, copies of contracts, etc. An appendix allows you to show flair and can help a fiscally small indie with a big reputation seal a deal.

Sample Business Plan for a Start-up Indie

This three-year business plan assumes the owner is not seeking external financing and does not plan to pull a profit from his venture until the third year. It is designed for an indie that is more of a hobby than a business; therefore, it shows how simple a business plan can be. While it is not designed to gain funding, this marketing plan does provide a road map for the owner and the people he hires, plus it gives bands an idea of what type of support the label plans to provide. If this label were to grow, it would need a more detailed business plan. The larger the financial risk, the more detailed your business plan must be.

By the way, Cherub Records and the individuals and bands in the sample business plan do not exist.

Business Overview

Mission Statement: Cherub Records exists to provide a Northwest-based audience with access to CDs by local goth and ethereal bands.

Audience: Cherub Records' primary audience are fans of Northwest goth music. Our secondary audience are national fans who become aware of our bands through national tours, airplay, media, or word-of-mouth. Our tertiary audience are international fans who become aware of our bands through media or word-of-mouth. In particular, the audience will be fans of the bands Lilly of the Valley, Chronic, and Gother Than Thou (GTT).

Market: There are currently no indies serving people interested in Northwest-based goth music. The Northwest goth scene is thriving, however. Lilly of the Valley and Chronic are already into second pressings of their self-released debuts. In addition, engineer/producer Mercy McGoth is making the best of the unique sound of each of the bands at Rusted Iron Studios.

Business Structure: Cherub Records is a sole proprietorship that plans to become a limited liability company after this three-year business cycle is completed.

Marketing Strategies

Distribution: Initially, the owner will conduct all distribution by contacting and following up with independent record stores in the Northwest. In addition, we will try to attain a regional distributor based on the strength of the bands and the record sales of Lilly of the Valley and Chronic.

Promotions: Promotions team will consist of publicity and radio promotions. Gina Rock will handle publicity while the owner will work radio and retail. Gina will send the records to select music publications across the country. She will follow up with those publications to make sure they received the records and to see if they plan to review the records, run a show preview, or run a story on the band. The primary concentration will be on Northwest publications. Gina will provide a list of the publications to be contacted for our approval. The bands will be responsible for their own tour promotion. The owner will send the record to select radio stations across the country. He will also follow up with those stations within a month to make sure they received the record and to see if the record is receiving any airplay. He will also try to arrange on-air interviews and performances with the band. The primary concentration will be on stations in the Northwest. A list of all stations that will be sent promos is included in the appendix.

Gestalt: Since we want to present a consistent image and sound, all label artwork will be done by J. L. Dark and, with very special exceptions, all recording will be done with Mercy McGoth at Rusted Iron Studios.

Audience: After we establish a solid and profitable regional base, we will expand to include the entire West Coast market and then try to break through on the East Coast. For the next three years, however, our concentration will be on the Northwest. We are assuming our audience fits the following description:

- They like and frequently go see Lilly of the Valley, Chronic, and Gother Than Thou
- They are either college students or work in the arts or the tech industry
- They purchase most of their records at shops that either specialize in or stock a large variety of goth albums
- They go to dance or music clubs several times a month

Competitive Analysis: Since there are no other labels releasing Northwest goth, we need only distinguish ourselves from national labels such as Cleopatra. What we have that they don't is the hometown advantage and the unique sound that comes out of Rusted Iron Studios. Our listeners can see these bands on a monthly basis and have an automatic dedication to our bands since they are part of the local goth community.

Operating Procedures

Recording: All recording will be done by Mercy McGoth at Rusted Iron Studios. Cherub Records will purchase a one week block of time for the band to record their record. The band is responsible to come into the studio prepared. This means that they will have done the following:

- Determined what songs they will record in what order and have practiced those songs for at least twenty hours in the past two weeks
- Predetermined the tracks designations and beats per minute
- Repaired their instruments—no humming amps, etc.
- Purchased necessary accoutrements such as strings, picks, sticks, and batteries

Pressing: Unless we find a company that offers comparable value for the price, Cherub will do all its pressing at Hot off the Press. We will provide both the artwork and the master to Hot off the Press simultaneously. We will request that they notify us of any problems with the artwork within two weeks, and provide us with proofs of the artwork within two-and-a-half weeks. We will specify that Hot off the Press should have our record delivered to us or our distributors within thirty days of receiving the artwork and master. All CDs will be placed in jewel cases and have a four-page CD insert, a tray card, and a CD label.

Artwork: All artwork will be completed by J. L. Dark on a freelance basis using the following criteria:

- He will use templates provided by Hot off the Press for CD inserts that he will have designed before the band finishes recording. He will receive all needed elements for the insert one month before the design is due. He will provide us with concepts one week after he receives the elements and a proof on the day the band starts recording. All CD inserts must include the following information: recording copyright notice; artwork copyright notice; song lyric copyright notice; trademark notice; credits for artwork and producer; songwriter and music publisher; Cherub logo, address, website address; catalog number and barcode.
- While the record is being pressed, he will also design a promotional poster for the band. He will receive all needed design elements two weeks before the band goes into the studio, provide

concept proofs one week after he receives the materials, and provide press proofs the week the band finishes recording. The posters will be sent to record stores and given to the band to promote shows.

Promotions: Our publicity team will consist of the owner and Gina Rock, a Portland-based national publicist. The owner will send records to select radio stations across the country immediately after it is pressed. In addition, he will follow up with those stations within a month to make sure they received the records and to see if the CD is receiving airplay. He will also try to arrange on-air interviews and performances with the band within two weeks of the record being released. The primary concentration will be on stations in the Northwest. A list of all stations that will be sent promos is included in the appendix. Gina will send the records to select publications across the country within two weeks of receiving it from the label. She will follow up with those publications to make sure they received the records and to see if they plan to review the records, run a show preview or story on the band. The primary concentration will be on Northwest publications. Gina will provide a list of the publications to be contacted for our approval. The bands will be responsible for their own tour promotion.

Distribution: Initially, the owner will conduct all distribution by contacting and following up with independent record stores in the Northwest. While the record is being pressed, he will try to get advanced orders by sending out an announcement of the record and a one sheet [see Chapter 9: Distributing Your Product] to regional record store buyers. Once the initial shipment CDs arrives, he will ship advance orders and promotional posters. All initial orders must go out on the same day so no record stores feel shafted. After the first shipment is sent or dropped off, the owner will personally visit all record-store buyers who did not make an initial purchase, give them a promo and a one sheet and either get an order on the spot or follow up with a request for an order within a week. All deliveries must be recorded and a receipt for the number of CDs taken will be presented to the buyer. The owner will follow up with all record stores on a biweekly basis to see if they need new stock. It is assumed most records will be purchased on consignment.

Personnel

Owner: The owner has spent the last five years working retail at various Portland-based record stores. He has also hosted a local music show at a college radio station and booked bands at various local nightclubs.

External Resources: In addition to the assistance of Gina Rock, producer/engineer Mercy McGoth and artist J. L. Dark, the owner will be working with a yet-to-be-named music attorney and an accountant who will also act as controller/financial advisor.

Gina Rock: Gina Rock worked for three independent and two major labels before striking out on her own as an independent publicist. Her clients have included artists who have made it onto the CMJ charts. She likes working with new bands and continuing to support them as they grow and gain national recognition. Since she lives in Portland, she has the respect of the local press, plus her national recognition will allow her to effectively promote the bands on a national level when the time comes.

Mercy McGoth: In addition to playing bass in the band Gother Than Thou, Mercy McGoth engineers most Northwest goth records at his studio, Rusted Iron. He produced the debut records for Lilly of the Valley and Chronic, both of which are in their second pressing.

J. L. Dark: In addition to designing the artwork for Lilly of the Valley's debut, J. L. Dark has designed covers for local magazines and his work has been displayed at Northwest galleries.

Financial Data

General Investment Budget: Assuming the owner keeps his current job, he will be able to sustain a loss of $12,000 annually. If the label does not succeed in breaking even within the first three years, the owner will disband it. The primary financial goal is to break even by the third year of operation.

Estimated Start-up Costs: Start-up costs for Cherub Records will prove minimal. Since the label will be run out of the owner's parents' basement, which is where records will also be stored, overhead is minimal. In addition, the owner will use his personal computer to conduct business. Estimated start-up costs include:

Start-up Costs

Trademark research (on Micropatent website)	$ 70
Trademark registration	$ 245
Accountant to Set up bookkeeping system	$ 500
Website registration	$70
Website design	$ 300
Logo, stationery, and business card design	$ 250
Phone installation	$ 60
Total start-up costs	$1,495

Estimated Operating Expenses: These expenses are divided into overhead expenses, such as phone bills, stationery, office supplies and production expenses, such as contract assistance, pressing, distribution, royalty fees, and promotions.

Annual Overhead Expenses

Local business license	$ 20
County business license	$ 40
State business license	$ 60
Legal assistance	$ 500
Phone bill (estimated at an average of $200 a month)	$2,400

Stationery and business cards	$ 500
Miscellaneous office supplies (estimated average of $50 a month)	$ 600
Estimated quarterly taxes (none until the label pulls a profit)	$ 0
	$4,120

Cost Per Initial Release

Sound recording registration	$ 30
CD design	$ 75
Poster design/printing	$ 250
Studio/engineer	$1,800
Tape costs (during recording process)	$ 500
CD pressing and insert printing (1,000 copies)	$2,500
Publicity for three months	$ 600
Mailing	$ 250
	$6,005

Projected Income From Initial Pressing

Income from the sale of 750 CDs at $7 apiece	$5,250
Production fees	$6,005
Royalty fees	$ 0
	$−755

Projected Cost/Income for Second Pressing Expenses

Pressing and Insert Printing (1,000 Copies)	$2,500
Deficit from first pressing	$ 755
Royalties at 11 percent (from the sales of 793 CDs after costs are recouped)	$ 611
	$3,866

Income

Income from the sale of 900 CDs at $7 apiece	$6,300
Expenses from second pressing	$3,866
Profit	$2,434

Second pressings are viewed as a windfall during the first three years.

Projected Annual Income and Expenses

Year	Start-up Costs	Overhead	Release #1	Release #2	Release #3	Total
One	$1,495	$4,120	-755	-755		-7,125
Two		$4,120	-755	-755	-755	-7,385
Three		$4,120	-755	-755	-755	-6,385

Financing

If you're a corporation that wants financing, don't give away your ownership. Keep the largest percentage of the stock you are selling. Ultimately, keeping ownership allows you to have a lot of say in the decision making of your business.

—Tess. Lotta

Since the music industry is notoriously unstable, it proves quite difficult to find investors, so plan to start with your own funds and seek alternative sources of financing—such as angel groups or production and distribution (P&D) deals—in the long run. The chance of getting a bank loan for your small business proves slim. Another funding option is to open a personal line of credit and draw from that as needed. This type of an emergency account comes in handy when you happen upon a hot-selling record and need to press up another batch pronto. Keep in mind that interest rates add up and it's usually a bad idea to finance your indie on multiple credit cards with a 21.7 percent interest rate. Once again, advanced planning for potential success proves key.

External investors and P&D deals provide two additional financing options. Investor angels are flush individuals interested in financing small businesses. It's best to meet them through other small businesses, however, they also advertise in newspapers and via the Internet. Keep in mind that individuals with cash don't come without strings. If they're financing something as risky as an indie label, they are looking for something in return.

If you want outside bucks, you need to work with someone with a finance background. Investors will want to review your current and projected financials, your primary staff, and your marketing plan. They're also going to want to know what sets your label apart from others and why it's going to provide them a return on their investment. To prepare for this, start working with an accountant early on. She can help you make decisions that will appeal to investors in the future. You will need to project your expenses, set sales and profit goals, and prepare a preliminary balance sheet (what you owe versus what you own). Unless you have experience developing marketing plans, it's advisable to work with someone that does. The Small Business Administration (SBA) has regional development centers that provide learning opportunities. They also offer help through Service Corps of Retired Executives (SCORE), (www.score.org), an organization that hooks novice business owners up with retired executives. While the SBA does not generally make loans, it guarantees loans to business unable to obtain financing through traditional sources. In other words, it is somewhat like a guaranteed student loan. In order to qualify for these loans, your label must demonstrate the potential to make a profit. In truth, SBA support outside of regional development centers and SCORE is unlikely for most labels.

P&D deals come in a variety of forms, the most simple of which involves delivering the finished product and art to a larger label that presses and distributes the CD. After they recoup their expenses, the larger label takes a percentage of the sales and gives you the rest. More complex deals involve advances to offset the cost of recording and promotions or reducing their percentage the larger label takes as sales of the CD increase. Whatever the deal, have your lawyer review it.

7 The Recording Process

A recording is never going to sound like the band does live. It might sound better, it might sound worse, but it will definitely sound different.

—*Nabil Ayers*

Making a CD is far more than plopping down band members' bottoms in a studio and letting them play as the tape revolves lazily around the sockets of a reel-to-reel recorder. The approach one takes to production is an essential component in creating the identity of a label. Outside of bands, producers (or in many cases simply engineers) are the most significant element in forming a label's sound. Although sticking to one producer or type of band is not necessary, varying too widely will muddy a label's vision. Most strong labels focus on a particular genre of music. People know what to expect and are willing to fork over more than a few bucks to take a chance on an unknown artist simply because a label they respect deemed the outfit suitable to release. Without this type of following, it is hard for a label to survive.

Depending on the genre, there may be one to a dozen major producers who create unique but similar sounds on a national level. Additionally, there are probably at least a handful of engineers who yield a similar vibe in any given community. They prove the most cost-effective alternative when a label is developing a regional following. While innovators who have the creative vision, technical torque, and plain luck of timing to spearhead a revolution pop up infrequently, lots of producers/engineers are more than capable of coaxing the best from a band. Look for a healthy combination of specialization and good people skills. You should have the same, which is why this chapter focuses on:

- producer and/or engineer selection
- studio options and elements
- financial and artistic benefits of pre-production
- home recording
- mixing
- mastering
- format options

Selecting a Studio and Producer

75 percent ears, 25 percent equipment!
—Jack Endino, on balancing equipment and the talent
of the people who run it

Many smaller studios have specific producers, or at least engineers, attached and vice versa, so young indies often purchase a package deal. While you can find relatively inexpensive studios, it is important to consider the folks running the equipment. A decent sixteen- or twenty-four-track studio will *start* at $200 a day, and that is if you cut a deal by booking a large block of time. Remember, if you're unhappy with the finished product, bargain basement prices can prove costly indeed.

People

Producers and engineers are the most important aspect of recording. Both the band and the label should feel comfortable working with the individuals selected. Any moneyed wannabe can purchase the latest in high-tech equipment, but an audio genius can coax a unique sound out of simple gear, not to mention bands with a willingness to learn. Surprisingly, many of the latter are not particularly expensive, especially if they are interested in pursuing a vision with the artists rather than cranking out product to pay the bills. Try to find someone with a good balance of altruism and business sense; she will inadvertently benefit your label. A decent business person will show up on time, work quickly, and troubleshoot effectively, which saves money in the long run.

If you're a small label with a limited budget, consider forgoing a producer and utilizing a studio with a top-notch engineer who has done decent work on other recordings. Often, the only difference between an engineer and a producer occurs at the more "sophisticated" levels of recording. Major labels hire producers to make an artist appeal to the broadest audience possible, which can have very little to do with bringing out the best in their sound. Even though bands often think they are self-produced, many a well-known genius launched his career by producing groups under the guise of being a simple knob-monkey. Growing with someone can prove rewarding to all parties concerned.

Who Chooses the Producer?

Sometimes the label has very specific ideas of who the band should work with, like it or not. Labels usually disagree with a band's choice of producer for creative reasons, not money reasons.

—*Jack Endino*

Ideally, a label and a band share a common vision, so this question does not come up too often. On occasion, however, a group wants a producer that is not conducive to the direction in which the label wants to take them. Usually the label wins, or the band walks away—unless they are under a contract and the indie chooses to hold them to it. Don't count on getting a top-notch record from that move, however. Unhappy bands generally make crappy, or at best sarcastic, records.

Long-term contracts usually only happen with majors or large indies and involve recording advances. Theoretically, advance money belongs to the band. In reality, the label decides how an artist spends it. A band sees no money until after the label recoups its costs. A much more common scenario is that the band shells out the bucks for recording and a label pays for pressing. On occasion the label will pay for recording and let the band select their own engineer, as producers are not often involved at the one-off (record contract) level.

Different Ears for Recording, Mixing, and Mastering?

It is sometimes desirable to have a person with "fresh ears" mix the record with the band so the producer/engineer who recorded it can get some distance. In other cases, the performances and sound on the tape are great, but the record company wants someone with a more commercial bent to mix the record so radio will like it (you know, turn the vocals up really loud, compress the heck out of it. Some producers are okay with this, some don't like it, but that's the biz. Mastering is the final stage, and the producer should be involved but it is less necessary.

—Jack Endino

Recording is where you want to invest the bulk of your money. This means the initial recording, the mixing (adjusting, manipulating, and tweaking sounds and sound levels), and the mastering (preparing a recording for mass reproduction). In most cases, one engineer/producer does all three. A separate person *can* be hired to create a mix, and on occasion, a master, however. Major labels routinely bring in engineers who specialize in mixing to create an accessible (read: generic) radio sound. Since most indies cater to music fans who are seeking anything *but* a generic sound, special mixing engineers are brought in to enhance, rather than revamp, what the recording engineer helped the band create.

Atmosphere

We were singing in a bathroom and there was a sewage problem. The bathtub was filled, but the record came out sounding great. It is certainly nice to be in a $1,000 a day studio where you can

send out for food and people are waiting on you, but this was a
zero dollar a day studio and it was fine.
                        —Nabil Ayers, on recording Micro-Mini's first full-length

Hammering it out live in front of an audience and recording a CD are two distinctly different experiences. Therefore, it is important that a band be comfortable not only with the producer but also with the atmosphere of a recording studio. Many bands bring in items from home or their practice space to cozy up their surroundings and make themselves feel at ease. This may sound cheesy, but creating art in the sterility of a studio is a challenging task. Then again, some studios come with a built-in atmosphere, also something to consider during the selection process.

Digital or Analog?

Retro purists and classical music lovers know analog recordings sound "warmer" than those that are digitally produced, but most people lack an understanding of how either system works. Here's the difference. Analog systems convert the electrical currents emitted by instruments to a magnetic pattern that is stored on tape then cut into vinyl. When one plays vinyl, the turntable converts the magnetic patterns to electrical currents that come out of your speakers as sound waves.

Digital recording stores sound waves in a binary form. Sound waves can be graphed and the digital process records music by storing the location and the order of all the points of a sound wave. A producer can now "warm up" the sound of a digital recording during mixing by running it through any number of contraptions designed to replicate analog warmth in a digital process. Although warming processors keep improving, the best way to get true warmth is to record at an analog studio.

How Many Tracks?

Although technology can prove seductive, more is not necessarily better. A new band can easily become overwhelmed during its first serious outing in a studio. When recording a young duo or a three-piece, consider the eight-track option. It will preserve the simplistic beauty of the ensemble and save the label from spending money on a studio for which a band is not ready. Sixteen- or twenty-four track studios allow a group to dedicate at least six tracks for drums, two tracks for guitars, and a track apiece for the bass and vocals. This leaves six to fourteen tracks with which a band can play; for example doubling the sound of a certain instrument to make it fatter, adding delay to thicken a sound, or providing more mics for the drums or additional instruments.

If you do stick a young band in a big studio, make sure they have an excellent rapport with the producer and engineer. They'll need to have a significant number of choices explained to them. Many musicians with years of self-recording experience on an eight-track get lost when shoved into a twenty-four-track studio. Besides, Nirvana's *Bleach* was recorded on a high quality half-inch eight-track and it sounds just fine.

Preproduction

> *Blue Note paid its bands to rehearse before they recorded, it saved time and money in the studio.*
> —Marty Jourard, technical columnist and former studio owner and keyboard player for the Motels

As previously mentioned, decent studios start at about $200 an hour and a band can waste a significant portion of their budget deciding song order, length, and final arrangements when recording on-site. The answer? Have the group make these choices at practice. Last minute changes are inevitable, but having the bulk of preproduction completed prior to recording will spare the bank account of whoever is paying for the project, not to mention prevent the band from breaking up in the studio. It's tough to keep cool heads when making selections at $200-plus per hour.

Other decisions that can save valuable pennies include predetermining track designation, deciding the optimum beats per minute for each song (with the help of an electronic metronome or drum machine), investing in necessary equipment repairs (read: no humming amps or tired drumheads), and purchasing basics such as strings, picks, sticks, and batteries.

Home Recording

A lot of people track stuff at home and mix it someplace really great. It takes a while to know how to make things sound good, but it is certainly possible with experience.

—*Nabil Ayers*

With the advent of the ADAT, a label can set up their own recording studio for about five grand. You need an ADAT eight-track recorder, a mixing board, monitors, microphones, and a DAT mix-down deck. Initially, you record to a VHS video cassette, then mix the songs down to DAT.

So if you can set up your own studio for a mere five grand, why not do it? Because you still need the ears. Small, label-owned studios are great for recording demos and helping a band prepare to record with a good engineer. Additionally, if an individual in the group has good production skills, she can create an album worth pressing on their own. Just keep in mind that not every band has a technical genius, and even if it does, that person still has to develop proficiency.

Mixing

Mixing people are like midwives. They may not know how to record or engineer, but they know how to mix. It is an art.

—*Marty Jourard*

Every song can be mixed an infinite number of ways, so if you use an additional engineer for the process, make sure you like his sound. It will have a definite effect on the end product. On the other hand, even the best mixing person cannot pull a recording from the grave. An original made with shoddy equipment will always suck. Don't expect the mix to fix it.

The basics of mixing include deciding how loud an instrument will be as well as how much of the sound will come out of the left and right speakers. Generally, the drums lay the foundation for the mix. Each is adjusted individually; then come the bass, guitars, horns and additional instrumentation, followed by the vocals. All are individually adjusted for tone and volume.

With the help of signal processors, many effects are also added during the mix, including reverb (creating acoustic depth), digital delay (creating echo), and compression (balancing, or limiting, the dynamic range), to name a few. For example, reverb is rarely recorded because it cannot be removed. Instead, the sound of the guitar is sent to a signal processor that creates its own output (in this case echo) that acts as an additional instrument in the mix.

Mixing can also take various segments of different takes of one number and patch them together to create the "perfect" song. It's akin to refurbishing a car from spare parts. Listen to a recording of Mariah Carey or Janet Jackson for the final effect.

After receiving several mixes, listen to each on a variety of sound systems. Other people will. If you think everything sucks, which happens, have the record remixed. After you make final selections, request copies on reel-to-reel or 1630 tape. DAT tapes can prove unstable. A final note on mixing: If you run out of money, don't necessarily settle on a mediocre mix. Consider saving your pennies and finding an engineer with whom you and the band are more in tune. A record lasts forever.

Mastering

> The mastering labs in L.A. have totally flat speakers that don't hide anything. "The horrible truth," is what the Motels called them. These are acoustically flat, special speakers. Whatever is on the tape is what comes out.
>
> —Marty Jourard

Major mastering labs in towns like L.A., New York, and Nashville start at three hundred bucks an hour. If that tidy sum exceeds your budget, consider a local mastering facility, which will do the same thing, with less spiffy equipment, starting at about $40 an hour. Once again, it is mostly in the ears, although equipment *is* important.

But what exactly does mastering do? At the very least mastering cleans up the crud between tracks. It can also provide cross-fades, increase or decrease the silence between two songs, and get rid of those nifty little pops. The engineer simply snips the pop from a graph on a computer. Additionally, equalizing, the major function of mastering, removes sounds below or above a certain frequency. Don't like the vibration of a truck passing by on that quiet acoustic track? Presto, it's gone. But the dog yelping along with the vocalist has to stay; unfortunately they're performing in the same register. On arrangements where each instrument is in its own frequency range, you can raise or lower a specific frequency in the mix. Finally mastering can compress a track and provide consistent volume.

Mastering can correct mistakes mixing is unable to rectify. For example, bands occasionally end up with no low- or high-end because the shape of the studio in which the music was recorded created a live sound not captured on tape. Mastering can doctor the recording by boosting or lowering certain frequency ranges. Mastering can also balance the discrepancies in sound created when an artist records at several different studios. These instances, along with basic clean-up functions, are how indies best put mastering to use.

Selecting a Format

> When you put out a band's CD, it's a big deal. That is their CD and it's their CD for a while—until their next one come out a year or two years later. A single is an in-between thing. No one's career is riding on it.
>
> —*Nabil Ayers*

Numerous elements influence the decision of whether to put out a single, EP, or full-length recording. Often a band's readiness to release a full-length is a larger issue than budget. On the other hand, deciding whether to record material on vinyl or CD is pretty simple. The only people who purchase vinyl are collectors.

Full-Length or EP CDs?

Although major labels release CD singles for some acts, they are a bit superfluous on the indie level. Their primary purpose is to promote a specific song to mainstream radio stations. Most indie label play is limited to college and community radio, so don't waste your money. When you need to press a CD single to promote an album, you'll know it; most stations program from full-lengths anyway.

EPs are a different story. While fans generally prefer to purchase full-lengths because they're a better value, it may prove beneficial for a band to release an EP on their first or second outing. It takes the pressure off. Artists in a studio for the first time will inevitably devour a large part of their recording budget simply learning how to make a record. Opting for an EP allows them to record a selection of songs and boot the ones they don't like before mixing. Alternatively, the group can choose five of their best songs and hammer them to perfection. This, of course, all depends on the label's (and the band's) approach. If you put out punk rock, it might be best simply to have the band set up and slam through their set live. It's sloppy, but pure.

The reason for releasing a sophomore EP has to do with material. While fans and the press expect their idols to churn out magic on demand, the truth is creativity just doesn't work that way. It requires a balance of hard work and inspiration, the latter of which occasionally takes time. Fan expectations are especially high if a group had a strong debut. Here's the catch. The primary songwriter(s) for a group may have spent five years writing the numbers on their first record. Within a year, they are expected to hop in the studio and produce the equivalent—if not better. That is, of course, on top of touring and doing press to promote the debut. In these cases less is definitely more. A few brilliant cuts can be lost in a sea of mediocrity and the press is fickle enough not to give a band another chance on their third release.

Vinyl or CD?

Collective Fruit gives artists 10 percent of the pressing of a single to sell at shows. That's how bands are usually paid for providing a label with a single. It puts the format into perspective. Unless you're a purist, forget vinyl. It's not practical. Those who love the shiny black discs will press them regardless. Vinyl lives on only because fanatics keep shoveling the dirt from its shallow grave.

Vinyl lovers fall into several categories: fans of obscure punk rock, indie rock, hip-hop, classical, and jazz, plus DJs. If your primary goal is to have a record played in dance clubs, a vinyl EP is the format most likely to catch a DJ's eye. Since DJs are serviced by labels, they purchase few records. The people that *do* purchase vinyl are collectors; therefore, it's important to select a band that appeals to them. Even vinyl singles from semifamous bands often sit on the shelves because, in most cases, the group's fans simply don't own turntables. Additionally, the few distributors who pick up singles do so only because they love the format. They are by necessity extremely selective in the vinyl they procure. Most singles are sold at the back of a club after a gig or through mail order. Certain labels (most notably Sub Pop in the mid-1990s) have a solid rep and collectors purchase any single they produce. It is a great way for the listener to sample a band. In all other cases, a performer needs to have both an established audience and one which is predisposed to purchasing vinyl to make pressing a single worthwhile.

Building Relationships

> *Well, part of the producer's job is to get along with people, and if he can't cut it he should excuse himself. Then again, some bands can be jerks in the studio; but in that case, the producer doesn't have to put up with it (life's too short!) and again, should excuse himself unless he craves the abuse.*
>
> —Jack Endino

Like everything else in the music industry, successful recording ventures rely on relationships. Since the recording process cuts to the heart of someone's artistic output, it is the area where relationships are most important. A band *must* feel comfortable with the people recording, mixing, and mastering its record. Labels can nudge, recommend, or at times step in and demand, but allowing an artist to exercise their vision is the reason most indies exist. If huge battles consistently erupt between a band and a label over recording, perhaps the match just isn't right.

8 Pressing and Packaging CDs

If I could tell bands one thing, it is don't book your CD release party before you have the CD.
  —Mimi Crocker, sales manager of DiscMaker in Seattle, Washington

Where do CDs come from? The shiny, space-age discs belie their production process. CD pressing plants are huge and, to a certain extent, imprecise beasts that pump out thousands of discs daily. Add to that the complexities of printing booklets, compiling the entire package, and delivering the product, and the process become rife with possibilities for potential snafus. In this chapter we will explore:

- The production process
- Packaging
- Design
- Print lingo
- Working with artists, models, and art
- Selecting a manufacturer
- Costs
- Timing

The Production Process

Surprisingly, five steps exist between your mastered recording and a mass-produced CD. First, the data is transferred from the master to a glass master, from which a father is produced. The mother is then separated from the father to create a stamper that begets a clear disc that transforms into a CD-ROM disc. So when did producing a CD become a family affair and just what is the purpose of all these various steps? Read on.

A glass master is a disc made from ground glass and coated with photoresist into which a laser etches the data from the master recording. After the etching, the glass master is coated with silver, then electroplated with nickel that is peeled away to make a negative known as the father. In theory, one could use the father to stamp CDs, but it would wear out quickly. To prevent having to repeat the costly steps necessary to recreate the father, several mother plates are created. Each mother plate can produce a number of stampers that press the data onto a clear disc. These are produced en mass and then covered with a thick layer of aluminum, which is what is read by the CD player. The information is protected with a lacquer coating and art and information, such as song titles, which are screen or offset printed onto the CD. Although offset printing costs about twice as much as screen-printing, it produces an image similar in quality to a photograph.

Manufacturers also stamp a particular lot number on each CD for quality control to make sure all CDs end up in the correct cases and with the proper art. The quality control process also checks to make sure each CD plays properly. Damaged CDs, along with the speed at which a press operates, accounts for the necessity of potential overages or shortfalls in pressing.

Packaging

Economy packaging could potentially limit your distribution. The other disadvantage is that consumers might resist paying a full-

*length album price if they're not getting a booklet with pictures
and the lyrics.*

—Mimi Crocker

Although the packaging options for CDs continue to expand, it's important
to remember that retailers prefer jewel cases, digipacks (one-piece cardboard cases with plastic trays), or eco-wallets (trayless one-piece pouches).
If you select another option, retailers may avoid stocking your CDs
because they do not fit neatly into their display shelves. That said, a variety of inexpensive packaging options exist for those who plan to sell their
CDs only over the Net, through the mail, or at shows and festivals. They
include die-cut jackets (a plain black or white cardboard carton with the
center cut out), clear vinyl jewelpaks (a thin two-fold vinyl packet that
holds a CD on one side and an insert on the other), and seashells (clear,
hard vinyl packaging that allows you to see the CD).

Design

When creating the artwork for a jewel case, make sure you remember to
develop a CD insert, tray card, and CD label. The are also special considerations when using a clear CD tray. The image that lies beneath the
CD must match or complement the cover of the tray card because a
quarter-inch strip will show through on the left-hand side. Check out any
clear CD case for clarification.

CD inserts come in a variety of sizes and configurations, the most
common of which include a four-page fold (folded in half), a six-page
gatefold (folded in thirds), an eight-page accordion fold, an eight-page
gatefold (two sides open to expose two panels with a fold in the middle),
an eight-page double fold (folds in half and then in half again with the
seam to the left), an eight-page poster fold, a ten-page double gatefold, a
twelve-page poster fold, and stapled booklets.

The tray card shows through the back of the CD. This is most likely
where you will include your songs' titles, label name, contact information, copyright and performance right information, and the all-important
bar code that will consist of twelve numbers. The first six digits are your

manufacturer's ID number. The next five identify the release, and the final number is a verification code. The same number—minus the small number to the right and left—will appear at the top of the spine followed by the artist's name, the release name, and the label name, in that order. You can start the process of acquiring a bar code by contacting the Uniform Code Council (see Appendix).

The CD label consists of whatever images and words are screened or offset printed onto the CD itself. At a minimum, this should include the artist or band and label name. Many industry folk find unlabeled CDs frustrating. If they get separated from the jewel case and the individual is unfamiliar with the artist's work, it is hard to match the two.

Finally, if an independent artist, rather than the CD manufacturer, creates a mock-up, run it by the pressing service to make sure it's the correct size. This simple step will prevent you from paying for the hand packaging of materials that fail to fit the machine, or worse, from having to run the entire print job over.

Print Lingo

Print lingo is as convoluted, confusing, and complicated as that which accompanies music production. Here are a few terms you'll need to know when working with designers:

Airbrushing: retouching artwork with color; traditionally performed with a small handheld sprayer but now done (like everything else) on a computer

Back printing: printing on the reverse side of a piece of paper

Color separations: the process of separating the colors of an image into cyan, magenta, yellow, and black film filters so it can be transferred to a plate that stamps the colors onto paper during the printing process

Color transparency: a fancy name for a color slide

Offset printing: a printing process that uses cyan, yellow, magenta, and black to create a full-color image similar to a photograph;

also called process color, four-color, and full-color

Prepress: the process of mechanically or digitally preparing a piece of artwork for printing

Nonreproducible color: colors in a piece of artwork that cannot be accurately reproduced in the printing process

Spot color: a single color added to the printing process

Working with Artists, Models and Art

Just as you have legal rights to the songs you pen, an artist has rights to his creative work and an individual has rights regarding the commercial use of her image. What this means is that you must make agreements with your artist regarding the use of his work, get clearance if your designer borrows art from another source, and score a model release from the pretty puss who graces the cover of your CD.

It is important to clarify your expectations with a designer. Lots of folks assume that if they purchase a piece of artwork it is theirs, which is not necessarily the case. In addition, you need to protect yourself by assuring that your designer has gained clearance for all images used in the design. For these and multiple other reasons, it's important to develop a contract when working with a designer. Necessary elements include:

- The type of services you expect, both art and prepress
- The expenses you plan to cover, such as supplies, photography, etc.
- The expectation that he will acquire copyright clearance and model release forms
- The types of rights you are purchasing; for example, you can buy the art outright, or pay only for the right to use the artwork on a CD
- The payment arrangements for the artwork, for example, half up front and half upon acceptance by the printer

While lifting old artwork is common among pop culture designers, keep in mind nothing published after 1923 is automatically in the public domain and is probably protected by copyright. For example, Sub Pop had to shelve the distribution of a TAD album because they borrowed and mutated the Pepsi logo on the album artwork. Having to recall an album due to artwork costs a lot in shipping, printing, and assembly.

The use of a person's image is also sticky territory. Make sure you, the photographer, or the graphic artist procures a model release form. You as the business owner need to keep the original release form. Ten years from now when you rerelease a CD with the same image, the model who once thought mooning a camera was funny might not want his children to see those photos. A model release form can be a simple document that states the name of the band and the model, the right to make the proposed use(s) of the photo, a brief description of the photo shoot, and the amount paid to the model. Like all legal documents, no matter how informal, the model needs to sign.

Selecting a Manufacturer

Due to the complexity of the manufacturing process, it's important that you make sure what is included in a bid and how special circumstances will be handled. Ask the manufacturer for a complete bid and then specify that you prefer no additional charges to pop up unexpectedly. Basically, it's best to ask around and find a manufacturer with a good reputation rather than bargain basement prices. Customer service is key and it's pleasant to work with people who are willing to overnight a partial shipment of CDs to a record release party when the run is not totally complete. At a minimum, the bid should include the following elements, although they need not be specifically broken out unless you request:

- Glass master
- Father
- Mother
- Stamper
- Clear disc
- Screen printing

- Delivery
- Jewel box or other form of packaging

Many manufacturers also offer design services. Unless you're doing strictly pressing and distribution for a band that supplies camera-ready artwork, it's best to have your own designer create CD artwork to maintain a consistent image. However, you might want to check out what type of work the company's design department has produced in the past. If you work with your own designer, make sure he or she gets specific dimension specs and that the company is willing to work with him to produce a quality product. Some manufacturers provide templates. If you hire a new designer for this process, make sure he is familiar with the printing process. Someone with a knack for creating good looking files on a design program does not necessarily know how to prepare a file for press, which could lead to an array of unattractive outcomes. If you use the manufacturer's design services, make sure the bid includes the following elements:

- A specific number of revisions to make sure you like the design
- The details on color (process color, spot color, or black only)
- The CD inserts
- The back printing
- The tray card

Another element to discuss is overruns and underruns. The industry standard is 10 percent in either direction. Due to the imprecise nature of CD production, when it comes to pressing and the weeding out of damaged CDs during the quality control process, a manufacturer cannot guarantee a precise number of CDs. You will always be charged for the additional CDs you receive, but some companies won't discount the damaged CDs from your bill. Find out up front what their policy is and negotiate not having to pay for product you do not receive.

Costs

The cost of a CD package can vary dramatically depending on what type of services you choose, not to mention the reputation and reliability of the manufacturer. Remember, problem-solving requires time and problem-solving equals customer service. If you go with a cut-rate outfit make sure you know their reputation. Here is what you might expect to pay for various types of CD packages from a reputable firm. Costs include pressing, insert, tray card, and jewel case. CD production costs are constantly dropping and it costs less per CD the more you press.

CD Production Costs

Type of Insert	Price Per CD					
	500	1,000	2,000	3,000	5,000	10,000
Full-color 1page	$1.86	$1.37	$1.29	$1.20	$1.05	$0.94
Full-color 4 fold	$2.07	$1.48	$1.34	$1.24	$1.06	$0.95
Full-color 6 fold	$2.42	$1.61	$1.40	$1.27	$1.11	$0.98
Full-color 8 fold	$2.53	$1.66	$1.43	$1.29	$1.13	$0.99

Timing

As a label owner, you owe it to your band to have product available for their tours (at least a first pressing). Of course, a band needs to understand they cannot book their tour until they are sure the record will be out and distributed. This can prove a lot more complicated than it sounds. It requires the synchronization of CD production, tour booking, and distribution. Some highly efficient companies can turn a CD package around in two weeks given that no unforeseen problems arise. This is rare. In reality, it's safest to allow at least a month for CD pressing. Distribution is a more complicated matter as you are usually relying on a middle man to sell your products and get them into stores before the performers' clunky van pulls into town. Bands check record stores to make sure their product is in stock when they tour. And of course they get rightfully peeved when it is not. If you can't sell to record stores in the cities where your bands are touring, make sure they take a couple of boxes along and be prepared to ship CDs to the group in case they run out. More details on this next to impossible polka dance are available in Chapter 11: Timing and Touring.

9 Distributing Your Product

You have to do your research and make sure we distribute your type of music. Ask other labels, ask vanity-distributed bands, and ask your favorite record store. If more labels did that research all of our lives would be a lot simpler. We're an independent alternative music distributor.

—Alicia Rose, president and part-owner of NAIL Distribution in Portland, Oregon

distribution proves a full-time job. Not only must a label possess the right products and eventually score at least regional distribution, someone must continually follow up with the stores that stock their records and shops in which they want to place their product. Most indies start with local distribution and eventually hook up with a regional distributor. Some even score national distribution, although this proves far less common.

Starting Out Small

A label can help themselves by getting into local record stores. Not every label needs a distributor. There has to be a demand for the record.

—Alicia Rose

Unless you snagged a well-known act out of the gate, most new indies need to start the distribution process locally. This means compiling a list of which record stores in your city carry the type of music you release. If you don't know most of them off the top of your head, stop and think whether or not you are really enough of a music fan to dedicate endless hours nurturing an indie because the buyers in the store will know if you're not. They are far more likely to purchase product from a bloke who regularly haunts their store looking for the latest releases than a complete stranger. After breaking into local record stores, you can expand to other shops in the regions in which your bands play. Once that exceeds two states (depending on the size of the state), it's time to look for a regional distributor.

It's generally best to approach a retailer in person. Call ahead to check when the buyer works and ask if it's okay to drop by (an appointment might be a bit formal), then pop in with a promo of your record. If possible, suggest a particular track for the buyer to listen to on the spot. If they don't have time, ask for a good day to make a follow-up call to get their opinion. In any case, make sure you have several CDs on hand in case the person wants to take them on consignment on the spot. Yes, consignment. You can try to sell your product outright, but your chances of success are minimal.

Before you visit local shops, prepare a one-sheet. A one-sheet should include a brief synopsis of the band's history including their previous releases, tour history, and airplay and chart history, if one exists. In addition, a one-sheet provides the band's promotional plans and most important, a description of their sound. Remember to include your address, fax number, phone number, and Internet and Web addresses. Make it short and snappy. A one-sheet serves two purposes: first, to get the buyer to listen to the record, and second, to convince the buyer that placing the record on his shelves is a sound investment. Once the buyer takes the records, present him with a written summary of what he has taken and have him sign it. Since many small record store owners are not organized, you must be.

Once you place product in the stores, check on it frequently. Stop by physically at least once a month to see how the CDs are selling and ask the buyer if she needs more stock. Remember that many retailers retain ownership of CDs if you fail to reclaim them within a certain period of time. This prevents dilettantes from dropping off records and not following up on a regular basis. Small record stores do not have time to baby-sit dozens of labels and bands.

Distribution Companies

> *People have a misconception about indie distributors. If they are picking you up, you're literally just a number in a catalog. Everything else is up to you. They just make it available in stores.*
>
> —Nabil Ayers

Once your bands attain regional recognition, it's time to seek out a regional distributor to sell your records to mom-and-pop (independently owned) record stores, chain stores, and one-stops. One-stops sell individual records (rather than boxes of records) to mom-and-pop stores. Although distributors do not generally require exclusive contracts, it's best to avoid overlapping areas so your records don't get stale. Larger regionals often work with other distributors to accommodate bands with an expanding market.

Three levels of indie distribution exist. The first level sells to mom-and-pop stores within a specific region. At this level, it's good to monitor your sales at pacemaker (trend-setting) stores to determine if your market should expand. Since pacemaker stores change frequently, ask your distributor who they are. The second level of distribution expands regional distribution by adding more regional distributors or having your current distributor work with other regional distributors. The third level involves hooking up with a major indie distributor like Caroline or RED. Of course, before you can jump to the second or third level, your band must warrant broader distribution and you must possess the means to press enough records to keep product in stock. In addition, using a distributor does not free you from retail promotion; in fact, it increases your responsibility. Now you need to contact stores outside of your region and the distributor as well. Details on retail promotion are available in Chapter 10: Promoting Your Product.

Terms and Shipping

> *People need to know that it takes forever to get paid and that you are going to get returns.*
>
> —*Nabil Ayers*

Indie labels frequently feel like distributors hang on to their hard-earned cash for far too long, but in reality, distributors are merely protecting their interests and preventing themselves from going out of business due to high returns. Distribution usually follows one of the five following paths:

First path:
- You send the product to the distributor
- The distributor sells the product to stores, kinda (basically, the retailers can return what they don't sell)
- The store sells the product and places another order
- The distributor sells through on your shipment and pays you

Second path:
- You send the product to the distributor
- The distributor sells the product to retail stores
- The store sells the product and places another order
- The distributor sells through on your shipment and orders more records
- You receive payment and send the distributor another order

Third path:
- You send the product to the distributor
- The distributor sells the product to retail stores
- The store sells the product and places another order
- The distributor sells through on your shipment
- You choose not to repress the record, but have a new release, and start the process over

Fourth path:
- You send the product to the distributor
- The distributor sells the product to retail stores
- The store does not sell all the records, but chooses to hold on to them indefinitely
- The distributor pays you for the records that have sold through, but retains 25 percent for potential returns from retailers

Fifth path:
- You send the product to the distributor
- The distributor sells the product to retail stores
- The store does not sell all the records, but chooses to hold on to them indefinitely
- You decide to recall the records so they do not sit on shelves
- The distributor recalls the records, credits the store for what has not sold, pays you for what has sold, and returns the remainder of the records to you.

Ideally, you have a string of records that sell through consistently. That way, the 25 percent distributors regularly retain to cover returns won't dramatically effect your ability to run additional pressings of a successful record. Payment terms can vary from thirty to ninety days after invoicing, depending on the agreement you make with a distributor. Since distributors, like labels, struggle with cash flow, smaller labels may sometimes receive payment late because they prove a lower priority than larger indies. By keeping shipments small, you can reduce sell-through time and keep the cash flowing.

As with all retail distribution, shipping follows a distinct protocol. First, expect to pay for freight both to and from the distributor. When shipping to the distributor, include an invoice with a distinct number for tracking purposes and the order number the distributor supplied when requesting the records. The invoice also needs to list the number of cartons shipped and the items in each carton. Include a packing slip that allows the distributor to check off merchandise when unloading. If you ship several boxes, note which one includes the packing sheet on the outside of the box.

Bankrupt Distributors

Distributors frequently go belly up, often in batches when the indie industry faces a downturn. Like many other industries, the popularity of independent records crests like a wave, and when a particularly large wave hits the beach, the infrastructure designed to support a specific genre or region gets smashed in the process. During these downturns—and often in isolated incidences—stock disappears and labels don't get paid. This can happen even if you know who you are working with, but there are some basic safeguards a label can take. If your distributor doesn't pay you, don't send them another batch of records. If they don't pay a lot of other people, don't send them the first batch of records. In other words, use common sense and listen to your instincts.

10 Promoting Your Product

A good publicist will work to get your band the appropriate kind of publicity, like coverage in local/college papers or free weeklies when you're out touring. She also won't promise you things she can't deliver, like a review in Rolling Stone *or a cover story on a national magazine. Basically, a publicist should support what you're already doing. Don't trust someone who promises that press in the right outlets will make your career.*
— *Scott Frampton, editor of* CMJ New Music Monthly

More than any other part of the music industry, promoting is about relationships, because the one thing everyone in the entertainment business shares is a lack of time. Records stack up in postage bins, on desks, and on top of the CD player. And despite a buyer's, editor's, or music director's (MD) best intention, there never seems to be enough time to listen to them all. A phone call from a well-trusted promotions person can alert an overwhelmed individual that an exceptional CD is coming, and a follow up call to make sure that individual received and had a chance to listen to a release makes sure a record gets its just desserts. While radio, print, and retail promotions all require specific methods, the types of people who succeed in promotions share several attributes. They're not afraid to pick up the phone, they know when to back off, they're methodical, they know how to read people, and most important, they're charming. In the end, good promotions is a matter of finesse.

If you're a one-person label, it's important to hire good outside publicity and promotions. Why? Because you probably have a day job. Even if you don't, calling people across the country on a consistent basis takes time. This means looking at call sheets and tracking who has done what with a record on a daily basis, then repeating the drill. It takes hundreds of phone calls to grow an artist and a record. In addition, it's your job to take guff from crabby program directors (PDs), music directors, overwhelmed retail folks, and grumpy editors.

Finding the Right People

Most indie publicists and firms only take on clients they deem worthy. In general, they aren't trying to fill your ears with crap.
—*Scott Frampton*

Finding a good promotions or publicity person can prove a tad difficult. The industry is full of hacks quite willing to take your money and do little to actually promote the record. Call a large college radio station, magazine, or retailer you respect and ask for recommendations. If possible, hire a national rather than a regional publicist or promotions person. When, and if, the time comes, they can take your record to the next level. Ask the individual for a game plan. How do they promote records both locally and nationally? In addition, you want to know if they specialize in a certain genre of music, with what artists they have previously worked, and what they have been able to achieve for those artists. Remember that just because someone scored the cover of your favorite magazine for the Red Hot Chili Peppers does not mean they'll do the same for your best friend's knock-off band. Small indies are best served by hiring independent folks who specialize in pushing breaking artists. Hiring fancy, large publicity firms in New York and Los Angeles proves a waste of your hard-earned cash because the folks at alternative papers tune them out when looking for breaking artists.

Once you nab someone you trust, let them do their job. Follow their suggestions for mailings, tour promotions, and conferences. If one of your bands is playing a major conference, pay part of your publicist's or promotion person's cost of attending. Other expenses you can plan to shell out for include long-distance charges and mailing. Finally, even the best promotions or publicity person can't perform miracles. In the end, no amount of good promotions can make a dud explode.

Radio Promotions

> *To me credibility and honesty is one of the most important things. That is something that is built over a period of time and that is what increases your contacts. They trust and believe you.*
> —Al Moss, owner of Al Moss Promotions

There are two primary types of radio stations, commercial and noncommercial. In the future, Internet stations will undoubtedly demand attention, but at the present time the number of folks with both the technology and the interest in listening to music via the Net proves quite limited. Still, it can't hurt to keep an eye on who reports to the CMJ Internet charts and occasionally call the stations regarding their listenership.

Types of Stations

Unless a station airs a specialty show that concentrates on either local music or a specific genre, most new indies can forget about attracting the attention of commercial radio stations. Commercial radio stations are large, centrally operated businesses looking for ratings. Period. The more people listen, the more they can sell the ears of those people to their advertisers. As a small indie, you probably lack product with the star power to attract the drones that listen to mainstream radio that often pipes in national programming and hires local DJs to add flavor. Since the FCC deregulated stations, the competition for airtime has gotten even stiffer. One company can own several stations in one city and more or less control, along with other radio conglomerates, what the general public hears. They conduct market research to determine which songs to play and spin primarily, if not exclusively, major label acts.

Even in instances where the music and DJ are live, a program director preselects the songs a jock spins. There are always exceptions, however.

Some stations have local music shows or specialty shows that actually take risks on breaking acts. Gaining the attention of the folks who run these programs requires either an established fan base or a previous relationship with the individual running the show. If you lack that relationship, try and work with an independent promoter with established contacts. In any case, sending CDs to the program director of stations who play genres similar to the ones you release can't hurt. In the music industry, miracles frequently do happen.

Noncommercial radio is generally college or community-based and far more open to new acts than their commercial counterparts. To effectively break a band, labels should familiarize themselves with all the stations that play the genres they release. This includes college, community college, high school, and general community stations. Even noncommercial stations generally require DJs to play a specific number of cuts from records in rotation. A record enters rotation when a music or program director deems it worthy of special note. Generally, rotation is broken into high, medium, and low sections. DJs must play a certain number of cuts from each section per hour. They fill the leftover time with songs from the station's library or their personal stash; therefore, it's also important to mail copies of a record to DJs who spin the genre of music you release. If a music or program director adds your record to rotation, ship extra copies to the PD and ask him or her to pass them on to interested DJs. It is also important to send copies of a record to DJs that host specialty shows that concentrate on your genres. These shows often highlight new artists that fail to score regular rotation.

Promoting a Release

Radio promotion is a tough gig and breaking a record nationally takes time as well as tenacity. As with most things, it's easiest to break a band locally, then move to national territory. The drill runs as follows: you mail out the CDs with a one-sheet. (A one-sheet should include a brief synopsis of the band's history including their previous releases, their tour history, and most important, their airplay and chart history. Remember to include your address, fax number, phone number, and Internet and Web addresses.) After the stations have time to receive and listen to the release, follow up to see if they have done either and let them know why this specific band would appeal to their audience. For example, they have strong local draw at clubs or the lead singer and songwriter fronted one of last year's flavors of the month. Once a local specialty show or station picks up the records, add that tidbit to your promotions arsenal. For example, the fact that KGRG in Auburn, Washington, plays cuts from your CD an average of three times a day might encourage other stations to add the record to their rotation. Once additional stations add the record, you not only have to break into other stations, but contact the program director at KGRG to let him or her know the record is hot and continues to get expanded airplay across the region or country. This keeps the CD in the station's rotation bins for a longer period of time. Complete a follow-up mailing if necessary and take advantage of touring bands to book on-road interviews and further push the record. Proper radio promotion demands consistent attention and a willingness to grow a band to their full potential through repeatedly updating program and music directors on how well the record is doing at other stations.

Charting

The independent music industry in the United States is interested primarily in the charts of two publications, *The College Music Journal (CMJ)* and, to a certain extent, *Billboard. CMJ* offers a series of weekly reports based on U.S. and Canadian college and noncommercial radio reports and other key industry indicators. Charts include the Top 200, AAA (Adult Album Alternative), Beat Box (Hip-Hop), RPM (Dance), Jazz, Loud Rock, N Alternative (Latin), New World (World Beat), and Internet broadcasts. Charts are available on-line or in the *College Music Journal* (see Appendix).

Billboard offers an array of charts, the most recognized of which is the Billboard 200, "the most popular singles and tracks compiled from a national sample of Broadcast Data Systems radio play lists and retail stores, mass merchant and Internet sales reports collected, compiled and provided by SoundScan," according to the publication's website. Soundscan is owned by *Billboard* and tracks and provides an array of information regarding entertainment sales.

Billboard album charts include the Billboard 200, Top R&D and Hip-Hop, Top Country, Pop, Heatseekers (up and coming artists), Independents, and Internet sales. Singles and airplay charts include the Billboard Hot 100, Modern Rock Tracks, Hot Rap Singles, Hot Country Singles and Tracks, Hot Dance Music and Club Play, Hot R&D and Hip-Hop Singles and Tracks, Adult Top 40 and No. 1 in Billboard. The AB Boxscore reports top-grossing concerts.

The charts you will most likely be interested in include Independents (obviously), as well as Heatseekers and any genre-related charts that might relate to your label. The Independents chart tracks titles sold by independent distributors while Heatseekers charts top-selling titles by up-and-coming artists. Once an album hits number 100 or above on the Billboard Top 200, they are disqualified from the Heatseekers list. Billboard charts are available on-line or in *Billboard* magazine (see Appendix).

Print and Internet Magazine Publicity

> In radio promotion you have to prove that there are the sales numbers. In publicity, most of the time, you are allowed to show your love for the music. But it's getting increasingly difficult. A lot of the print magazines that used to cover good independent music have changed their direction and cover things that sell in order to expand their base.
>
> —Barbara Mitchell, owner of Deluxxe Media

Like radio promotions, publicity takes persistence and tenacity. Luckily, many on-line magazines, small zines, and free local publications constantly search for fresh material and faces. Your first bits of attention will more than likely come from these sources. In addition to on-line zines, college papers, alternative weeklies and monthlies, some local daily papers also acknowledge new talent. Although most well-known progressive national music publications ignore bands without a strong regional buzz, there are always exceptions. Send the record to everyone and remember to follow up—even if it means just leaving a message on the answering machine of a person who won't take your calls.

Types of Publications

In order to send CDs to the right publications, you must know their audience. In addition to on-line publications most indies need to hit college papers, zines, and free weeklies and monthlies.

As the number of people with personal access to the Internet continues to increase, so does the importance of the medium. Currently, however, the Internet primarily serves the middle class and above. While most folks have access to the Net either through school, work, or the public library, only a limited percentage have the time to trudge to the library or are willing to risk losing their job to cruise their favorite on-line rag. So, if your primary audience is middle class, make sure to familiarize yourself with the sites that cover your genres and check out how many hits they receive daily. Otherwise, wait awhile. One day people will stash as many computers in their homes as they do televisions.

If your music serves folks in their early twenties, college papers provide an excellent outlet. Students not only frequent clubs, they blow their disposable income on CDs. When researching college papers that cover the type of music you put out, don't forget to include junior and community colleges on your list of prospects.

Zines probably provide the best outlet for breaking acts. Since love of music rather than money motivates their publishers, they escape the pressure of providing proof of mass circulation to potential advertisers, so they cover who and whatever they damn well please. In addition, editors of zines dedicated to music search out new sounds and ideas. If you live outside of a major metropolitan area, you can write SeeHear, a New York City shop and zines distributor, for a catalog to help you identify indie publications that might cover your bands.

Free weeklies and monthlies provide another good outlet. Most boast extensive music sections that cover a wide variety of genres. Several ways exist for a small label to pitch stories to these types of publications in their hometown or region. First, of course, there are band stories. The angle can be anything from the fact that they have a good draw to something peculiar like the lead singer is a Russian immigrant who translates the philosophies of Ayn Rand into pop music. Trend pieces provide another option. For example, pitch a story that examines the huge underground rap scene in your city. Although the story covers the scene, a writer may interview you as an expert. In many ways, building a following for your label proves far more important than promoting one particular artist as label recognition benefits all your releases.

Remember to develop relationships with both music and arts editors. Find out what makes them tick. Does their wardrobe consist solely of rock T-shirts? Are they out on the town every night? Or do they sit at home surrounded by stacks of CDs and magazines? Every editor possesses her own way of sniffing out stories. It's your job to find out how to best reach them. Out-of-town editors prove a bit tougher. If you lack relationships with out-of-town weeklies and monthlies, contact the booking agent of the clubs your band plans to play and ask which editors and publications in town might run a story. Some clubs hire publicists to promote their shows. In those cases, find out if you can support their efforts with photos or product.

Some dailies provide fantastic music coverage while others run nothing other than Mariah Carey concert reviews. Outside of your hometown paper, you'll only score coverage in a daily when one of your bands plays the publication's town.

You probably won't receive national media attention unless either your label or the artist already possesses solid regional reputation. You can circumvent this conundrum by hiring a well-respected publicist who knows which national writers and editors might adore the CD and slip a review of the record into their publication. In addition, one never knows when an editor needs to fill a hole in their publication at the last minute. Having a good record in the right place at the right time can achieve miraculous results.

Publicizing a Release

Sometimes people miss a band the first time out. You have to show them that there is a reason that they should be covering this particular artist.

—Barbara Mitchell

Scoring initial awareness proves the most important step of the publicity process. Writers won't cover a release unless they know it exists. This might sound simple, but consider the endless bins of CDs all music editors receive on a weekly basis. Good publicity involves far more than mailing out hundreds of records and hoping an editor unwittingly takes note of the package. Truth is, of the records in those bins, at least half suck. Your first job is to demonstrate to an editor why yours doesn't. Most good editors take the time to spin at least a couple of tracks from every CD or have someone they trust do the same. This helps them pass the record on to someone with an expertise in the genre. Why is this a good thing? Because no one human likes all genres. For example, an editor who fails to fancy jazz might automatically forward all such releases on to his jazz expert without even slipping the CD into a player.

Say the editor likes the genre, but thinks the first two cuts suck. What gets them to the best track? Well, a press release that informs the editor that cut five is the CD's standout might help. A phone call stating the same might work as well. And don't be afraid to leave a message. Even if an editor refuses to take your calls, she might jot down a note about the CD, the cut, and honor your request.

Promotional toys tend to work with new editors but seasoned professionals just take the loot and run. They get scads of promotional items, so goodies are meaningless unless they tie directly into the release and help the editor remember it exists in the long run. For example, "Hey wasn't Soap Scum that band that sent us the package of scrubbing bubbles?"

In the end, nothing gets your record noticed more than name awareness or a good publicist. No matter how jaded the editor, certain labels just make him dive to the bottom of the postal bin, rip open the bubble wrap, and slip the disc into a player. A record by their favorite band, given if it is on a bad label, drives them to rip open every package from the source until they unearth the wanted booty, and a call from a drinking buddy/publicist will get a release a guaranteed spin. At the very least, take the time to make sure the editor received the release, and send them another copy if they let you know they didn't. After the initial mailing and phone calls, it's time to build on your success. Your initial press will probably be local. After you've built a good base, reservice regional and national outlets with an updated press packet that features clips of the most prominent local media, and remember to hit other regionals once the band starts to tour.

Image

While you probably won't outfit your bands in a new wardrobe, publicity does deal with a band's image. Often, a publicist must either build an image from scratch or overcome preconceptions. Building a band's image lets people know what they're about. Are they roots rock? Political hip-hop? Avant garde jazz? While most bands hate to be pigeon-holed, their image is what helps busy industry professionals sum them up in a nutshell. Like it or not, it's often what sells records.

Nursing a band past a negative image proves far tougher. The music industry is constantly in search of the next flavor of the month. Therefore, talking an editor past the perception that an artist is last year's—or worse, last decade's—news takes a lot of finesse. The same holds true for artists who previously played in bands of a now tired genre. The key to convincing a person that a performer has moved past their goth or sugar-pop roots, is getting them to listen to the record with fresh ears, and sending them clips in which other writers confirm the transformation.

Publicity Packets

A good publicity packet consists of a copy of the record or disc, a short bio on the band, a photo, and the release date. Nothing fancy. If it's too long, busy editors won't read it and we're not impressed by fancy folders and packages either.

—Scott Frampton

In truth, everyone has a different idea of what makes up a good publicity packet. Common elements exist, however. They include a brief bio, a good black-and-white photo, a limited number of clips, and most important, a good record, because in the end, it is all about the music.

Make sure the bio not only states what the band sounds like, but why they are relevant or interesting. What clubs have they played? For whom have they opened? What previous bands have the individuals played with? In addition to history, try to come up with something distinctive. Editors are always looking for fresh angles, so play up anything that sets the band apart from their contemporaries.

It's also important to invest in not only good photography, but in good photo reproduction as well. Many free publications as well as all daily papers use newsprint. Newsprint has a high absorption level, which means the ink bleeds. In other words, a drop of ink expands on the paper, so if your photo is dark, it turns out muddy. Not that you'll have to worry, because the paper more than likely won't run the photo. In fact, without a good quality photo, they might not even run an article. When selecting publicity photos, look for good contrast. Make sure that you don't shoot the lead singer in a dark purple shirt against a black background. If at all possible, spring for actual prints rather than digital reproductions, which have halftone dots. These dots conflict with the dots used in the printing process and cause a picture to look rough. It also pays to have color transparencies (slides) or prints. Printing in color is expensive, so when a publication springs for the process, they want to use it. If it comes down to putting one of two bands on a color page, the group with a color photo in hand has the edge.

With clips remember that less is more, at least to an extent. No one will shuffle through reams of clips, so compile your best five. In most cases, this means including clips from the five most notable publications. If the band received a well-written extended feature in any publication, you might want to include that as well. It shows that someone deemed the band worthy of extensive consideration.

Internet Promotion

All labels and bands need a website to let fans know about show and release dates. You can also sell product on-line. If you offer on-line purchases make sure you secure credit card orders to avoid someone intercepting a card number. A more simple option is to promote mail-order sales via the Internet or offer the record through other on-line sources such as Amazon.com.

Additional on-line opportunities include band chats and list serve for your label and your acts. Finally, a Web site should always act as a good resource for journalists, buyers, PDs, DJs, and A&R reps.

Advertising

Advertising is expensive so place it carefully. Genre-specific zines provide the best bang for the buck when selling records. For local publications, co-op advertising proves the best bet. You can run a co-op with a local or out-of-town club because they usually get a discount for advertising on a regular basis. You can also do co-ops with your distributor when your band is touring through a certain town. For the most part, radio advertising proves cost prohibitive; even major labels don't advertise on it.

In general, the bigger the ad you place, the more attention it will get. If you're shelling out the bucks for an ad take a look at the paper and request good placement. "Placement" refers to where in the publication an ad falls. Most publications charge for prime placement but try to accommodate the requests of people even if they don't pay an extra fee. If you frequently place advertising, you actually have a fair amount of leverage for good placement because the paper wants to keep your business.

Retail
Promotion

> *BMG supplied me with a listening station when I owned my record store, Music Menu. I signed a document that said I would put specific artists in it. They sent me eight artists per month. It was free promotion for me, which meant a lot.*
>
> *—Glen Boyd, sales, promotions, and retail guru*

Once your records are distributed, it's time to follow up with retailers about stock and the band's story. You can use good sales in one region to encourage a retailer in another area to put up a point-of-purchase display. Make calls at least once a month and, if the store promises to use it, send promotional materials. T-shirts are especially good because people who work in record shops tend to be broke. Remember to keep in touch with your distributor and let them know details about tours, sales, radio play, and media coverage.

Due to the slim profit margin for retailers on records, many charge for product placement. Which means listening station slots, window displays, and display units cost bucks. On the other hand, if a retailer has leftover space, they'll probably give it to their favorite indie, so make sure to have point-of-purchase material ready for the asking. Also, offer to have your band perform an in-store when on tour. It will not only sell records, but also boost attendance at their shows.

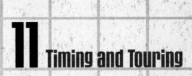
11 Timing and Touring

A band should have at least six weeks lead time to book a tour and a record in the stores before they start the tour.
—*Julianne Andersen, owner of AlphaFemale (MT) Booking*

booking a tour is a logistical nightmare in and of itself. Add to that the complications of getting the records into stores, and scoring radio airplay and newspaper articles in the cities in which the band is touring at the right time, and synchronicity proves almost beyond the grasp of mere mortals. That said, it takes the active involvement of distributors, retail and radio promotions, publicity, and booking to make a successful tour. In this chapter we will explore:

- Booking
  - Booking and negotiations
  - Tour seasons and regions
- Timing
  - Release dates
  - Distribution
  - Promotions and publicity

Booking

Booking a tour is an art form for which most agents receive grief rather than gratitude. Something goes wrong, and the band blames the booking agent, as does the label and sometimes even the group's fans. In truth, booking a tour proves so tough that disaster is bound to rear its head somewhere along the well-trodden paths the band's van treads on its way to live performances. For this reason, it is beneficial for a band to work with a reputable booking agent, if at all possible. Booking agents charge rates of up to 20 percent of a band's fee; however, they also know the market and have contacts that will save a band time and probably fetch a higher performance fee. In addition, an agent will knowledgeably review contracts and riders and perhaps prevent personnel at venues from treating a band badly, because the club's larger reputation is at stake in the industry.

Booking and Negotiations

Booking lead times vary drastically. They start at about six weeks and stretch up to a year, depending on the club or type of event. For example festival lead times are far longer than those of bars that host rock shows on Tuesday nights. If a band is self-booking, it is imperative that they have a list of venues that host their genre and the lead time of those venues before they embark on the venture. The actual process of booking a band at a club goes like this:

- Contact the venue, and offer to send them a promo kit
- Set a potential date for the gig
- Negotiate compensation
- Commit to a date

This process might sound simple, until you factor in venue lead time variance. The person booking the tour needs to set potential dates with numerous clubs within a particular region—or set of regions—while trying to achieve effective routing, because every night a band does not perform costs them money. In addition, many of the steps noted above require the individual performing the booking to dance a jig with the clubs.

Unless an individual has an established relationship with a club, it is best they leave an introductory phone call stating what time they plan to tour the region and offering to send a promo pack, including a CD, in case the person booking the venue is unfamiliar with their work. Once contact has been established and the promoter displays interest, a potential date for the show is set. That date is far from reserved. Clubs book several bands for each date. This allows them to score the best band possible while making sure a good draw night doesn't stand empty. Since a booking agent is also working to route a tour efficiently, they might request a date change from a venue. These two components result in club dates shifting and opening frequently. So what might be an empty date three weeks before a band leaves on tour will fill two days before it hits the road.

Once a potential date is set, a series of phone calls negotiates compensation. Compensation means much more than cash. It can also include a preshow dinner, a hotel, or even airfare to an international venue. After these details are hammered out comes the commitment. A commitment is always best done in writing. Preferably, the promoter or venue will send out a contract; if not, the individual booking the tour should send a confirmation letter.

Tour Seasons and Regions

Most tours happen during the spring and autumn months. Touring during the winter months results in vans flipping over on unfamiliar icy back roads and club attendance simply drops off during the summer. In addition, tours also take place in a particular region or set of regions. In the U.S., these regions include the West Coast, Mid-Atlantic, Northeast, Midwest, and the South. Europe is often cut into Northern Europe and Southern Europe because clubs in the North have a much longer lead time than the South.

Timing

Most label owners have one responsibility: have the product in stores on time so fans can buy it while they are amped up for, or by, the live show. In addition, a label can provide tour support in the form of publicity and promotions. If you plan to provide such support, make sure that you include it as an all-in (see Chapter Four: Music Law). In other words, stipulate that the record must recoup tour promotions expenses before the band receives royalties.

Release Dates

Records are released in one of four quarters that break out as follows:

- First quarter, January–March
- Second quarter, April–June
- Third quarter, July–September
- Fourth quarter, September–December

Traditionally, indies released their records during the first quarter because majors didn't. It was a quarter that music dilettantes quit buying CDs so they could pay off their holiday credit-card bills. Since die-hard music fans never stop buying records, this quarter allowed indies to target the die-hard market without having to compete with the majors. Indies now nab an increasingly larger share of the pie, so this wisdom has faded a bit. From a band's perspective, first quarter releases are great since they increase the possibility of their records being in stores when they tour in the spring, despite any pressing or distribution disasters. Plus you'll have to fight fewer major releases for review space in local and national rags.

If you release a record during the second quarter, it might not be in record stores for a spring tour if your pressing, sales, and distribution resources are shaky. However, students are in school and socially hooked in, so they are likely to hear about a record through word of mouth. Third quarter is a slow season for the music industry all around, although a summer release date will guarantee that a record will be in the shops for a fall tour. Records released during this quarter are often sleepers and don't gain attention until the fall when students share them with each other or until the band tours. If you're brave, you can release a record during the fall, but then the record may not be in stores for a fall tour, plus you'll have to fight a flood of major label back-to-school and holiday releases for review and article space.

Distribution

Many a band has headed out on tour to find record stores in some of the cities they play don't carry their CD. How does this happen? Pressing, sales, and distribution problems top the list of potential foibles. Since tours are booked at least two months in advance, a band takes a risk when booking a tour around the release date of a record. Thousands of indie records miss their release date annually. In fact, some indies miss their release dates by quarters rather than weeks or months. It is best to have the record in the stores before starting out on tour. Conventional wisdom says a CD should be in shops at least two weeks prior to touring. But considering that pressing and distribution can be delayed, earlier is always better. If you plan to release a record in February, and the band starts to tour in April, things are much more likely to go smoothly than if you plan that release for March.

It is the label's job to conduct retail promotion when the band is on tour. At its most basic, this involves getting the record into stores. Use the fact that the band is touring as a selling tool. In addition, contact record stores to see how the record sold around the tour and use that for additional leverage with stores who have not stocked the CD. Tour support can also extend into merchandising. Ask the record store if it will put up a poster or point-of-purchase item around the tour dates. This will both increase record sales and show attendance, which might in turn lead to more record sales. If the band and a retailer have the time and space, an in-store signing or short performance can be arranged.

You can also provide the booking agent or band with promotional posters that announce an upcoming gig. When the agent calls to confirm a gig, he or she can ask the person who books the club if they will place promotional posters up a week or two prior to a gig. If so, the agent or the label can send copies of the poster to clubs that do.

Even if you are, for some reason, unable to get the record into stores, make sure that the band takes plenty with them to sell at shows. That way fans can snatch up a copy if the local record stores fail to order or sell out of the CD. If your band releases an unexpectedly hot CD, be prepared for a second pressing and the likelihood of shipping copies to the band while they are on the road. For this and many other unexpected emergencies, a label should have a copy of the band's itinerary, whether they are providing tour support or not.

Promotions and Publicity

As if aligning gigs, release dates, distribution, and retail promotions weren't complicated enough, a label has to decide whether or not to provide a band with publicity and radio promotion for the tour. If the label can't chip in, a wise band will arrange for both prior to hitting the road. Folks won't come to a show if they do not know the band is playing. In addition to word of mouth, the way most people find out about shows is via tabloid ads and listings, radio tags, club calendars, and flyers for a show or a club.

Free local publications tend to be the medium of choice for finding out about shows. A tabloid can promote a show in several different ways, including a record review tagged with a show date, an up-and-coming preview blurb, a calendar listing, and a feature article on the band. In addition to publications having different lead times, they also have different dates for different types of coverage requests. For example, they may want three months lead time for a feature article, but the tour date faxed to their calendar editor two weeks before their press date. It is a publicist's job to know all the lead times for the various publications in different regions. Tour publicity involves a lot of information and coordination. A publicist needs to make sure the editor is familiar with the band in time for him to make a decision on whether or not to run a feature or preview on the act. In addition, they need to arrange for the writer to have necessary publicity materials before they interview the band, which is often on the road, and this leads to another coordination nightmare. Calendar editors often make decisions on blurbs based on how much space the calendar has to fill. If there are fewer listings, there are more blurbs. Therefore, it's always good to send this individual a press packet as well. If they end up with extra space at the last moment, a band whose information they have at hand is likely to fill it. If you can't get a preview, offer to put a writer on the list and ask for a live review. It won't pull people to the show, but it might help sell records. Finally, some clubs have their own press people, so make sure to send them any promotional material they need as they may have influence, or even be drinking buddies, with the editors at local publications.

Advertising a show in a local publication also raises awareness. One ad can advertise a band's album and show. The bigger the ad the better, and be sure to request good placement. Remember that publications also have ad deadlines, usually a space reservation deadline and a date the physical ad needs to be in their hand.

College and noncommercial radio also provide another good venue to promote a show. Most read on-air calendars of upcoming shows and events, host live performances or interviews, and most important, spin the record. A music-obsessed, volunteer DJ is pretty likely to mention that one of your bands is coming through town after she plays a song from the recent CD. If there are DJs that have a special interest in your label or type of music, send them a copy of the CD. Promoting touring bands to a college or community station probably means talking to several people: the music or program director to make sure the record is in rotation, the promotions director to coordinate give-aways for tickets or records and to make sure the date is on the club calendar, and the individual (sometimes the promotions director, sometimes not) responsible for arranging on-air performances and interviews. Once again, an experienced radio promotions person will know who to contact for what and when. Radio stations, like publications and clubs, all have different lead times.

Clubs offer additional promotion options. Many put up preview posters when they're provided. In addition, venues often place their own ads and send in calendar listings to local publications. You can also contact the club publicist, if one exists, and ask if the city in which they are located allows postering. If the answer is yes, arrange to have someone poster the town. Some clubs publicize their upcoming shows heavily while others do nothing, so you can't count on them to promote the show. If they do provide publicity, make sure to ask them how you can help.

Finally, don't forget band and label resources. If the band has a mailing list, send out a postcard containing their tour itinerary. Bulk e-mails do the same thing for less money and always, always, post tour dates on the label and band Web sites.

12 Selling Out

Good preparation—if you ever thought your company could be sold—is to understand the difference between two of the most important types of assets: Goodwill assets and physical assets. Your reputation is a goodwill asset, which you can try to quantify. A major record company should pay for your goodwill.

—Tess. Lotta

As an indie, you have two primary things to sell: your goodwill assets (or reputation) and your roster. In order to sell these items, your books must be in order and the business as a whole must present an attractive package to a major label, which will most likely be the entity absorbing your indie. Although you may have the most fantastic roster in Cleveland, an individual or corporation looking to buy your label will want to examine the following:

- Goodwill Assets
- Profitability
- Assets
- Liabilities

Goodwill Assets

Your reputation revolves around your label's relationships with suppliers, buyers, distributors, employees, and most important, bands and fans.

Theoretically, if you haven't got this, no one will look at you. There are exceptions, however. Sub Pop went through a heap of trouble and Warner Music Group still purchased 49 percent of the company for a reported $20 million. *This will probably not happen to you.* The label had such a strong roster that they survived reported late payments, late deliveries, poor stock tracking, and God knows what else. They also had Nirvana, whose rights they sold to pull themselves out of debt before Warner Music Group came a courtin'.

Since goodwill assets involve people, the buyer may want to guarantee that you and your primary staff—A&R, sales, and anyone else who makes the business run—stick around for a while. This is done in the form of a contract where the primaries of a company agree to stay for a predetermined amount of time, for which they usually derive some sort of monetary benefit.

Profitability, Assets, and Liabilities

A prospective buyer will want to review your current and projected financials, your primary staff, and your marketing plan. They're also going to want to know what sets your label apart from others and why it's going to earn them a truckful of cash after they buy it. Among other things a prospective buyer will want to see:

- An operating budget that details facility needs, promotional costs, projected supply expenses, utilities, labor, legal, professional, and royalty fees, as well as depreciation and projected income.
- A set of current and projected financials. Financials determine how much cash you need, project your expenses, estimate your revenue, and set up your sales and profit goals. They generally include a preliminary balance sheet, a list of assets (what you own) and liabilities (what you owe). If you have some liabilities tucked beneath the radar (like unpaid payroll taxes), a savvy buyer will find them. In terms of assets, they will review your inventory, equipment, furniture, leases, and perhaps determine if your current location

allows you room to grow. Any outstanding accounts receivable will be reviewed and analyzed for the likelihood of their collection. They may run credit checks on your customers.

- An implementation schedule that identifies how much money you will need and when.

You'll need to show that the label runs at a profit; basically, that your bands can sell enough CDs to pay the bills and have some money left over. If a record company purchases your indie, it might view things a bit differently. The bane of many indies' existences is that they have the right bands, but not enough money and distribution power to push them. A record company has plenty of both, so the fact that you have amazing talent and ears *may* make up for the lack of a cushy bank account.

Carrie Akre

After being signed to the now defunct Y Records in Seattle, Carrie Akre and her band Goodness signed to, and were dropped from, two major label subsidiaries: Lava/Atlantic and Immortal/Epic. Surviving those trials—which included Atlantic bringing in songwriter Stan Lunch—motivated the diva to launch her own label, Good Ink (www.goodink.com). Carrie started out her career as the front woman of Hammerbox.

Julianne Andersen

Julianne Andersen has been booking bands since 1990 and owns her own agency, Alphafemale Booking. She recently started the Tempest Project, an agency that conducts and coordinates booking, tour promotions, and retail promotions.

Nabil Ayers

Nabil has dabbled in almost every area of the music industry throughout his eight-year career. After completing a retail internship with Polygram in Seattle, he launched a label, Collective Fruit, and worked at an independent record store, Easy Street, in Seattle. He subsequently opened his own record shop, Sonic Boom (www.sonicboomrecords.com), with Seattle DJ and label-owner Jason Hughes. In addition to his retail and label ventures, Nabil has drummed in both indie and major-label bands including the Lemons, Micro Mini, and Alien Crime Syndicate (www.theacs.com). Nabil is also known for having the best sideburns in Seattle.

Glen Boyd

Glen has worked in radio, print, publicity, sales, retail, and marketing during his twenty-year career in music. In addition to hosting a rap program on KCMU, he has written for *Spin, The Source, Pulse!,* and *The Rocket.* He also worked as a publicist at Mirimar Records, acted as national sales director for Will Records (www.willrecords.com), owned his own record store, Music Menu, and served as national retail marketing director for Def Jam American/American Recording and NastyMix Records. Although Mr. Boyd works behind the scenes instead of in front of a mic, he has been known to leave a mean rhyme on his home answering machine.

Mimi Crocker

Sales and customer service manager of Disc Makers (www.discmakers. com) in Seattle, Mimi Crocker launched her career as an artist manager. She also owned and ran a small regional distribution company, Ivey Music Group, from 1993 to 1998.

Joe Ehrbar

Former editor of *The Rocket*, a bimonthly music mag in Seattle and current critic for the *Seattle Post Intelligencer*, Joe Ehrbar ran his own indie, Trench Records, from 1993 to 1997. When not writing, Joe listens to one of his twenty Wesley Willis records.

Jack Endino

An internationally renowned producer, Jack Endino "can't remember how many records he's made or how many countries he's worked in." Suffice it to say, Mr. Endino created the Seattle Sound as part-owner of Reciprocal Studios and the primary producer for early Sub Pop recordings. He also played in an array of bands, most notably his long-term projects Skin Yard and Endino's Earthworm. In addition, Jack maintains a website, www.jackendino.com, which offers everything from recording hints to critiques on the Kurdt Cobain books. Jack has an intense fear of canned ravioli.

Scott Frampton

Scott Frampton is editor of *CMJ New Music Monthly* (www.cmj. com/newmm/).

Marty Jourard

Best known as the keyboard and sax player for the Motels, Marty Jourard went on to own a recording studio and now writes a technical column for musicians.

Tess. Lotta

Tess. moonlights as an international bookkeeper to support her true calling as a musician, booking agent, and journalist. In addition to performing in cabarets, she played in Danger Gens, Maxi Badd, Algea, Megababe, and Bobbitt. Tess. also books an emerging talent night in Seattle and contributes to *BUST, Moxie, Instant Planet,* and *The Iconoclast* magazines. She once performed a piece titled "All this from a Lane Bryant nightgown minus the panties."

Barbara Mitchell

Before launching her own firm, Deluxxe Media, the mighty Ms. Mitchell worked as a publicist for Slash and World Domination, and freelanced for a variety of labels and marketing companies. Many of her purses have feet.

Al Moss

Owners of Al Moss Promotions in Texas, Al specializes in attaining alternative country and Americana airplay for established and breaking acts.

Alicia Rose

President and part-owner of NAIL distribution (www.naildistribution. com), Alicia Rose has also booked clubs, worked at five different record stores, and hosted a radio show on KUSF in Portland. Alicia performs avant garde ditties on the accordion as Ms. Mergatroid.

Vanessa Veselka

As owner of the small indie, Yeah, It's Rock (www.yeahitsrock.com), Vanessa introduced the world to the Valentine Killers and subsequently had a record that stayed on the CMJ Top 20 for sixteen weeks. A musician first and foremost, Vanessa started playing professionally as a fifteen-year-old runaway. Her work first appeared on a compilation titled *White Trash New York Folk Vol. 1* on 109 Records. Since that time she has played in Bell, which released records on Y as well as her own label, and a variety of additional projects.

Professional Organizations and Institutions

This listing is in no way an endorsement of the following businesses or organizations. Specific addresses, locations, and phone numbers may have been changed.

CONFERENCES

Association for Independent Music (AFIM) Convention
An annual conference held in Cleveland in May for indie retailers, distributors, and labels.

Main Office:
AFIM
P.O. Box 988
147 East Main St.
Whitesburg, KY 41858
Phone: 606-633-0946
Fax: 606-633-1160

New York Office:
AFIM
P.O. Box 465
114 Lark St.
Altamont, NY 12009
Phone: 518-861-7037
Fax: 518-861-7038

CMJ Music Marathon, MusicFest, and FilmFest
This New York-based conference hosts primarily alternative radio personnel each October. The four-day event includes panels, seminars, networking events, and shows.

CMJ
810 Seventh Ave., twenty-first flr.
New York, NY 10019
Phone: 646-485-6600
Fax: 646-577-0010

The Gavin Music Summit

This radio conference takes place
in August in Boulder, Colorado.
The four-day event includes
music, panels, speakers, and
presentations.

Gavin
140 Second St.
San Francisco, CA 94105
Phone: 415-495-1990
Fax: 415-495-2580

International Folk Alliance Conference

An annual festival held in
February in Vancouver, B.C. It
offers exhibits, courses, and
showcases.

Folk Alliance
1001 Connecticut Ave. N.W., ste.
501
Washington, D.C. 20036
Phone: 202-835-3655
Fax: 202-835-3656

MIDEM

A conference based in Cannes,
France, that includes a trade
show, showcases, and panels.
The conference is particularly
geared toward international
commerce and offers an
excellent opportunity to learn
about, and make contacts for,
international licensing
opportunities.

Reed Midem Organization (USA)
125 Park Ave., twenty-fourth flr.
New York, NY 10017

Phone: 212-370-7470
Fax: 212-370-7471

New Music West

A Canadian-based conference
that takes place in Vancouver,
B.C., in May and draws from
both sides of the border. In
addition to panels and
networking events, the
conference offers showcases and
an unofficial counter-festival
comically titled "Music Waste."

New Music West
1376 Seymour St.
Vancouver, BC V6B 3P3
Canada
Phone: 604-684-9338
Fax: 604-684-9337

NXNE

This Canadian-based conference
takes place in June and is
coordinated by SXSW. The
conference offers networking
opportunities, a trade show,
showcases, and panels for those
interested in the Canadian music
industry.

U.S. Registrants:
SXSW
P.O. Box 4999
Austin, TX 78765
Phone: 512-467-7979
Fax: 512-452-4775

Canadian Registrants:
NXNE
189 Church St., lower level
Toronto, ONT M5B 1Y7
Canada
Phone: 416-863-6963
Fax: 416-863-0828

SXSW

The big daddy of all conferences,
SXSW takes place in March and

is commonly acknowledged as spring break for the music industry. The conference offers networking opportunities, a trade show, showcases, and panels for those interested in the national and, to some extent, the international music and film industry.

SXSW
P.O. Box 4999
Austin, TX 78765
Phone: 512-467-7979
Fax: 512-452-4775

CHARTS AND PLAY LISTS

Billboard
Billboard magazine publishes charts derived from SoundScan sales figures, radio airplay, and concert ticket sales.

Billboard
770 Broadway
New York, NY 10003
Phone: 800-449-1402
Fax: 404-442-7998

Chart
Chart magazine publishes monthly Canadian charts based on college radio specialty airplay. Genre charts include electronic, metal, hip-hop, jazz, and world music.

Chart Communications, Inc.
#200-41 Britain St.
Toronto, Ontario M5A IR7
Canada
Phone: 416-363-3101
Fax: 416-363-3109

CMJ
CMJ offers a series of weekly charts based on U.S. and Canadian college and noncommercial radio reports and other key industry indicators. Charts are available on-line.

CMJ
810 Seventh Ave., twenty-first flr.
New York, NY 10019
Phone: 646-485-6600
Fax: 646-557-0010

Gavin
Gavin publishes play lists for more than 1,300 radio stations and fourteen formats. In addition to the Top 40, they report on rhythm, adult contemporary, urban, hot adult contemporary, alternative, AAA, country, Americana, rap, jazz, and smooth jazz.

Gavin
140 Second St.
San Francisco, CA 94105
Phone: 415-495-1990
Fax: 415-495-2580

Indie Music World
Provides indie wholesale and retail charts.

Indie Music World
P.O. Box 998
Whitesburg, KY 41858
Phone: 606-633-0946
Fax: 606-633-1160

Pollstar
Pollstar magazine publishes a chart detailing the box office of major artists.

Pollstar U.S.A.
4697 W. Jacquelyn Ave.
Fresno, CA 93722

Phone: 559-271-7900
Fax: 559-271-7979

INDEPENDENT DISTRIBUTORS

Action Music
Genres accepted: eclectic

Action Music
6541 Eastland Rd.
Cleveland, OH 44142
Phone: 440-243-0300
Fax: 440-243-4063

Alternative Distribution Alliance (ADA)
Genres accepted: eclectic

ADA
72 Spring St., twelfth flr.
New York, NY 10012
Phone: 800-239-3232
Fax: 212-343-2504

Associated Distributors, Inc. (ADI)
Genres accepted: eclectic, especially hip-hop

ADI
3803 N. Thirty-six Ave.
Phoenix, AZ 85019
Phone: 602-278-5584
Fax: 602-269-6356

Bayside Distribution
Genres accepted: eclectic

Bayside Distribution
885 Riverside Pkwy.
West Sacramento, CA 95605
Phone: 916-371-2800
Fax: 916-371-1995

BIE Records
Genres accepted: eclectic

BIE
722 N. Nineteenth St.
Allentown, PA 18104
Phone: 610-432-2893
Fax: 610-740-9744

Big Daddy Music Distribution
Genres accepted: eclectic

Big Daddy Music Distribution
162 N.E. St.
Kenilworth, NJ 07033
Phone: 908-653-9110
Fax: 908-653-9114

Big State Indie
Genres accepted: contact distributor

Big State Indie
3065 McAll Dr., ste. 4
Atlanta, GA 30340
Phone: 404-454-7866
Fax: 404-454-7757

Burnside Distribution, Corp.
Genres accepted: eclectic

Burnside Distribution, Corp.
122 S.E. Twenty-seventh St.
Portland, OR 97214
Phone: 503-231-0876
Fax: 503-231-0420

Caprice International Records
Genres accepted: eclectic

Caprice International Records
P.O. Box 808
Lititz, PA 17543
Phone: 717-627-4800
Fax: 717-627-SONG

Cargo
Genres accepted: eclectic

Cargo
1557 N. Honore St.
Chicago, IL 60622

Phone: 773-772-6005
Fax: 773-772-5344

Caroline
Genres accepted: eclectic

Caroline East
104 W. Twenty-ninth St., fourth flr.
New York, NY 10001
Phone: 800-275-2250
Fax: 212-643-5563

Caroline West
6161 Santa Monica Blvd., ste. 208
Los Angeles, CA 90038
Phone: 800-767-4639
Fax: 323-468-8627

Carrot Top
Genres accepted: indie and jazz

Carrot Top
935 W. Chestnut, ste. LL15
Chicago, IL 60622
Phone: 312-432-1194
Fax: 312-432-1351

City Hall Records
Genres accepted: eclectic

City Hall Records
101 Glacier Pt., ste. C
San Rafael, CA 94901
Phone: 415-457-9080
Fax: 415-457-0780

Com Four
Genres accepted: eclectic

Com Four
7 Dunham Pl.
Brooklyn, NY 11211
Phone: 718-599-0513

Creative Musicians Coalition
Genres accepted: eclectic

Creative Musicians Coalition
1024 W. Wilcox Ave.
Peoria, IL 61604
Phone: 309-685-4843
Fax: 309-685-4878

Crystal Clear Sounds
Genres accepted: eclectic

Crystal Clear Sounds
10486 Brockwood Rd.
Dallas, TX 75238
Phone: 214-349-5057
Fax: 214-349-3819

Cyclone Records
Genres accepted: contact distributor

Cyclone Records
24 Pheasant Run
Merrimack, MN 03054
Phone: 603-585-6435
Fax: 603-424-8289

Darla Records & Distribution
Genres accepted: eclectic

Darla Records & Distribution
3460 Potter LN
Sacramento, CA 95821
Phone: 916-973-1730

Distribution North America (DNA)
Genres accepted: contact distributor

DNA
1280 Santa Anita Ct.
Woodland, CA 95776
Phone: 800-910-8444
Fax: 530-661-7880

Drumbeat Indian Arts
Genres accepted: American-Indian music

Drumbeat Indian Arts
4143 N.J. Sixteenth St.
Phoenix, AZ 85016
Phone: 800-895-4859
Fax: 602-265-2402

Dutch East India Trading

Genres accepted: eclectic

Dutch East India Trading
P.O. Box 738
Syosset, NY 11791
Phone: 516-677-6000
Fax: 516-677-6007

Elegance & Zesty Record Distribution

Genres accepted: contact distributor

Elegance & Zesty Record
Distribution
8027 Thurston Dr.
Cicero, NY 13039
Phone: 315-699-5613
Fax: 315-699-7918

FAB Distribution

Genres accepted: contact distributor

FAB Distribution
598 Victoria C.P. 36587
St. Lambert, QE J4P 3S8
Canada
Phone: 514-465-2389
Fax: 514-465-7517

Festival Distributors

Genres accepted: blues, roots, folk, and world beat

Festival Distribution
1351 Grant St.
Vancouver, BC V5L 2X7
Canada
Phone: 800-633-8282
Fax: 604-253-2634

Get Hip Records

Genres accepted: punk and related genres

Get Hip Records
Columbus and Treble Aves.
Pittsburgh, PA 15233
Phone: 412-231-4766
Fax: 412-231-4777

Ground Level Distributors

Genres accepted: rap, R&B, and hip-hop

Ground Level Distributors
629 Sonora Ave.
Glendale, CA 91201
Phone: 818-550-9860
Fax: 818-550-0141

Hep Cat Records & Distribution

Genres accepted: rockabilly, surf, garage, soul, and early punk

Hep Cat Records & Distribution
P.O. Box 1108
Orange, CA 92856
Phone: 800-404-4117/714-490-5520
Fax: 714-490-5521

Imaginary Entertainment

Genres accepted: mainstream jazz

Imaginary Entertainment
5324 Buena Vista Pike
Nashville, TN 37218
Phone: 615-299-9237
Fax: 615-299-9237

Indie Productions

Genres accepted: electic

Indie Productions
P.O. Box 507
North Uxbridge, MA 01538
Phone: 508-278-5240

Koch International
Genres accepted: eclectic

Koch International
2 Tri-Harbor Ct.
Pt. Washington, NY 11050
Phone: 516-484-1000
Fax: 516-484-4746

Ment Media Group
Genres accepted: eclectic

Ment Media Group
P.O. Box 812
Tannersville, NY 12485
Phone: 518-734-6985
Fax: 518-734-6995

Mordam Records
Genres accepted: punk and related genres

Mordam Records
P.O. Box 420988
San Francisco, CA 94142
Phone: 415-642-6800
Fax: 415-642-6810

Morning Song Distribution
Genres accepted: Christian

Morning Song Distribution
14179 Killarney Rd.
Siloam Springs, AZ 72761
Phone: 800-621-3059
Fax: 800-982-7741

NAIL, Inc.
Genres accepted: indie music and related genres

NAIL Inc.
1620 S.E. Hawthrone Blvd.
Portland, OR 97214
Phone: 503-736-3261
Fax: 503-736-3264

Parasol
Genres accepted: pop

Parasol
905 S. Lynn St.
Urbana, IL 61801
Phone: 217-344-8609
Fax: 217-344-8652

Paulstarr Distribution
Genres accepted: eclectic

Paulstarr Distribution
1660 Lake Dr. W.
Chanhassen, MN 55317
Phone: 612-361-6667
Fax: 612-631-6936

Pulse Soniq Distribution
Genres accepted: contact distributor

Pulse Soniq Distribution
340 Bryant St., third flr. east
San Francisco, CA 94017
Phone: 415-957-1320

Priority Records
Genres accepted: eclectic

Priority Records
6430 Sunset Blvd., ste. 900
Hollywood, CA 90028
Phone: 800-235-2300
Fax: 213-856-8796

Qualition Imports, Ltd.
Genres accepted: eclectic

Qualition Imports, Ltd.
24-02 Fortieth Ave.
Long Island City, NY 11101
Phone: 718-937-8515
Fax: 718-729-3239

RED
Genres accepted: eclectic

RED
79 Fifth Ave.
New York, NY 10003
Phone: 212-337-5200
Fax: 212-337-5252

Redeye
Genres accepted: eclectic

Redeye
P.O. Box 4821
Chapel Hill, NC 27515
Phone: 919-929-7648
Fax: 919-929-7648

The Local Music Store
Genres accepted: eclectic

The Local Music Store
2800 Juniper St., ste. 1
Fairfax, VA 22031
Phone: 703-641-8995
Fax: 703-641-9254

Twinbrook Music, Inc.
Genres accepted: eclectic

Twinbrook Music, Inc.
227 W. Twenty-ninth St., fifth flr.
New York, NY 10001
Phone: 212-947-0440
Fax: 212-947-4567

Two Cool Productions
Genres accepted: country and
traditional

Two Cool Productions
310 E. Chicago Blvd.
Britton, MI 49229
Phone: 517-451-8259

GOVERNMENT AGENCIES

**Canadian Bureau of
Intellectual Property**
The Canadian Bureau of

Intellectual Property protects the
works of creative artists in
Canada and processes copyright
applications.

Bureau of Intellectual Property
Consumer and Corporate Affairs
Department
Ottawa-Hall, K1A OE1
Canada

**Copyright Office, Library of
Congress**
This government institution
protects the works of authors,
provides information on
copyright law, and processes
copyright applications.

Copyright Office
Library of Congress
101 Independence Ave. S.E.
Washington, D.C. 20559
Public Information Office: 202-
707-3000
24-Hour Forms Request: 202-
707-9100
Web site: www.lcweb.loc.gov/

**Occupational Safety and
Health Administration (OSHA)**
Sets and oversees safety and
health standards at businesses
that operate in the United States.

*General Industry Compliance
Assistance Office*:
Phone: 202-219-8031

Publications Office:
Phone: 202-219-4667
Fax: 202-273-9266
Web site: www.osha.gov

**Small Business Administration
(SBA)**
The SBA provides small
businesses with basic information
on operations. In addition to a

variety of written materials, they offer workshops and mentoring programs.

National Headquarters
409 Third St. S.W.
Washington, D.C. 20416
Phone: 800-U-ASK-SBA

U.S. Trademark Office

Issues trademarks and the forms necessary to file for them. Most forms are available on the U.S. Trademark Office Web site.

U.S. Trademark Office
Assistant Commissioner of Trademarks
2009 Crystal Drive
Arlington, VA 22202
Web site: www.uspto.gov

LICENSING ORGANIZATIONS

American Society of Composers, Authors, and Publishers (ASCAP)

ASCAP licenses music and collects royalties for the public performance of that music. ASCAP publishes a variety of manuals and a quarterly magazine, *Playback.*

ASCAP Marketing
1 Lincoln Plaza, sixth flr.
New York, NY 10023
Phone: 212-621-6000
Fax: 212-362-7328
Web site: www.ascap.com

ASCAP Licensing Office
2690 Cumberland Parkway, ste. 490
Atlanta, GA 30318
Phone: 800-505-4052
Fax: 770-805-3475

ASCAP Los Angeles
7920 W. Sunset Blvd., third flr.
Los Angeles, CA 90046
Phone: 323-883-1000

ASCAP Nashville
2 Music Square West
Nashville, TN 37203
Phone: 615-742-5000

Association for Independent Music (AFIM)

AFIM promotes all aspects of the independent music business. It also holds an annual conference in Cleveland.

AFIM Main Office
P.O. Box 988
147 East Main St.
Whitesburg, KY 41858
Phone: 606-633-0946
Fax: 606-633-1160

BMI

A music performing rights and licensing organization.

Web site: www.bmi.com/

BMI New York
320 W. Seventy-seventh St.
New York, NY, 10019
Phone: 212-586-2000

BMI Nashville
10 Music Square East
Nashville, TN 37203
Phone: 615-401-2000

BMI Los Angeles
8730 Sunset Blvd., third flr. west
West Hollywood, CA 90069
Phone: 310-659-9109

BMI Miami
5201 Blue Lagoon Dr., ste. 310
Miami, FL 33126
Phone: 305-266-3636

BMI Atlanta
P.O. Box 19199
Atlanta, GA 31126
Phone: 404-261-5151

Harry Fox Agency, Inc./National Music Publishers' Association

Harry Fox Agency clears copyrights to songs for a fee. They are the most common source for gaining copyright permission. The National Music Publishers' Association lobbies for copyrights and related issues.

Harry Fox Agency, Inc./National Music Publishers' Association
711 Third Ave.
New York, NY 10017
Phone: 212-370-5330
Fax: 212-953-2348

SEASAC

A music performing rights and licensing organization.

SEASAC
55 Music Square
Nashville, TN 37203
Phone: 615-320-0055
Fax: 615-329-9627

OTHER ORGANIZATIONS

American Tinnitus Association

Educates the public on the treatment and prevention of tinnitus.

American Tinnitus Association
P.O. Box 5
Portland, OR 97207
Phone: 503-248-9985

Association for Independent Music

In addition to sponsoring the Indie Awards, this organization provides resources for member indies and wholesalers.

Association for Independent Music
P.O. Box 988
Whitesburg, KY 41858
Phone: 606-633-0946
Fax: 606-633-1160

Association of Independent Music Publishers

This organization holds meetings and events to promote the exchange of information between indie publishers. Publishes *Indie Music World,* which offers charts and features.

Association of Independent Music Publishers
P.O. Box 1561
Burbank, CA 91507
Phone: 818-842-6257

Copyright Society of the USA

The Copyright Society of the USA promotes the study of copyright law. It also offers lectures, seminars, and lunches.

Copyright Society of the USA
1133 Avenue of the Americas
New York, NY 10036
Phone: 212-354-6401

H.E.A.R.

H.E.A.R. is a nonprofit dedicated to educating rock musicians on the dangers and prevention of tinnitus.

H.E.A.R.
P.O. Box 460847
San Francisco, CA 94146
Phone: 415-773-9590
Fax: 415-552-4296

Nashville Songwriters Association International (NSAI)

NSAI offers workshops to help songwriters of all genres protect their rights. NASI is a nonprofit organization.

Nashville Songwriters Association
1701 West End Ave., third flr.
Nashville, TN 37203
Phone: 615-256-3354
Fax: 615-256-0034

North American Folk Alliance

The North American Folk Alliance promotes a culturally diverse array of folk music, dance, and storytelling in North America. It also offers an annual conference in February in Vancouver, B.C.

North American Folk Alliance
1001 Connecticut Ave. N.W., ste. 501
Washington, D.C. 20036
Phone: 202-835-3655
Fax: 202-835-3656

Songwriters Guild

The Songwriters Guild is an educational and networking organization for songwriters.

East Coast:
Songwriters Guild
1560 Broadway, ste. 306
New York, NY 10036
Phone: 201-768-7902
Fax: 201-867-7535

West Coast:
Songwriters Guild
6430 Sunset Blvd., ste. 705
Hollywood, CA 90028
Phone: 323-462-1108
Fax: 323-462-5430

South:
Songwriters Guild
1222 Sixteenth Ave. S, ste. 25
Nashville, TN 37212
Phone: 615-329-1782
Fax: 615-329-2623

Uniform Code Council (UCC)

The UCC issues bar codes that allow companies to identify products and shipments worldwide.

Uniform Code Council, Inc.
P.O. Box 713034
Columbus, OH 43271
Phone: 937-435-3870
Fax: 937-435-7317
Website: www.uccouncil.org

Volunteer Lawyers for the Arts

Provides pro bono legal advice and free legal education for the arts community.

Volunteer Lawyers for the Arts
Headquarters
1 East Fifty-third St., sixth flr.
New York, NY 10022
Phone: 212-319-2787
Fax: 212-223-4415

PUBLICATIONS

Trade Magazines

Absolute Sound

Absolute Sound covers emerging technologies in recording. The publication offers equipment and software reviews and articles.

Absolute Sound
7035 Bee Cave Rd., ste. 203
Austin, TX 78746
Phone: 512-306-8780
Fax: 512-328-7528

Acoustic Guitar

Acoustic Guitar covers acoustic guitar trends, techniques, and artists.

Acoustic Guitar
P.O. Box 767
San Anselmo, CA 94979
Phone: 415-485-6946
Fax: 415-485-0831

Acoustic Musician

Acoustic Musician offers tips, techniques and artist profiles for players of acoustic stringed instruments.

Acoustic Musician
P.O. Box 1349
1065 River Rd.
New Market, VA 22844
Phone: 540-740-4005
Fax: 540-740-4006

American Songwriter

This publication covers the craft of songwriting as well as performing arts organizations and copyright law.

American Songwriter
1009 Seventeenth Ave. S.
Nashville, TN 37212
Phone: 615-321-6096/800-739-8712
Fax: 615-321-6097

Audio Media

Audio Media covers breaking trends, equipment, and software for recording, broadcast, and multimedia.

Audio Media
1808 West End Ave., ste. 906
Nashville, TN 37203
Phone: 615-329-1557
Fax: 615-329-1558

Bass Player

This publication provides tips and articles for bass players.

Bass Player Magazine
2800 Campus Dr.
San Mateo, CA 94403
Phone: 650-513-4300
Fax: 650-513-4642

The Beat

The Beat is dedicated to reggae, African, Caribbean, and world music.

The Beat
Bongo Productions
P.O. Box 65865
Los Angeles, CA 90065
Phone: 323-257-2328

Billboard

Best known for its charts, this weekly publication also reports industry, news, trends, and gossip.

Billboard
770 Broadway
New York, NY 10003
Phone: 800-449-1402
Subscriptions: 800-745-8922
Fax: 404-442-7998

Chart

A monthly Canadian-based magazine, this magazine publishes monthly charts as well as reviews and stories with up-and-coming bands.

Chart Communications, Inc.
#200-41 Britain St.
Toronto, Ontario M5A 1R7
Canada
Phone: 416-363-3101
Fax: 416-363-3109

CMJ

The alternative music authority, *CMJ* offers a variety of charts based on airplay and other key industry indicators. They also review releases and report on alternative music news and upcoming releases. The publication is available on-line.

CMJ
810 Seventh Ave., twenty-first flr.
New York, NY 10019
Phone: 646-485-6600
Fax: 646-557-0010

Dance Music America (DMA)

DMA covers information relevant to professional DJs including music, equipment, and news.

DMA
7943 Paxton Ave.
Tinley Park, IL 60477
Phone: 708-614-8417
Fax: 708-429-7830

DJ Times

This publication covers the equipment and music used by professional DJs.

DJ Times
25 Willowdale Ave.
Port Washington, NY 11050
Phone: 516-767-2500
Fax: 516-767-9335

Electronic Musician

This publication covers all aspects of recording a release including equipment, software, and multimedia.

Electronic Musician
6400 Hollis St., ste. 12
Emeryville, CA 94608
Phone: 510-653-3307
Fax: 510-653-5142

Gavin

Gavin reports on radio news and artists weekly.

Gavin
140 Second St.
San Francisco, CA 94105
Phone: 415-495-1990
Fax: 415-495-2580

Gig

This publication is dedicated to touring musicians.

Gig Magazine
Miller Freeman PSN, Inc.
460 Park Ave. S., ninth flr.
New York, NY 10016
Phone: 212-378-0400
Fax: 212-378-2160

Ice

Ice reports release dates and runs short stories on well-known artists.

Ice Magazine
P.O. Box 3043
Santa Monica, CA 90408
Phone: 310-829-2979
Fax: 310-829-2979

Modern Drummer

This publication is dedicated to drum equipment and techniques.

Modern Drummer
12 Old Bridge Rd.

Cedar Grove, NJ 07009
Phone: 973-239-4140
Fax: 973-239-7139

Performing Songwriter

Performing Songwriter covers
the art and business of
songwriting.

Performing Songwriter
390 Downing St.
Denver, CO 80218
Phone: 303-778-8977
Fax: 303-778-8975

Pollstar

A weekly publication dedicated
to touring, club, and concert
information. Content includes
industry news, gossip, prospects,
tour itineraries, and executive
and artist profiles.

Pollstar U.S.A.
4697 W. Jacquelyn Ave.
Fresno, CA 93722
Phone: 559-271-7900
Fax: 559-271-7979

Sing Out!

This quarterly publication
presents information on folk
songs and music.

Sing Out!
P.O. Box 5460
Bethlehem, PA 18105
Phone: 610-865-5366
Fax: 610-865-5129

Consumer Magazines

3rd Coast Music

3rd Coast covers roots and ethnic
music.

3rd Coast Magazine
620 Circle Ave.

Round Rock, TX 78664
Phone: 512-218-8055

Album Network

This publication provides a
weekly review of an eclectic
array of albums.

Album Network
120 N. Victory
Burbank, CA 91502
Phone: 818-955-4000
Fax: 818-955-8048

Alternative Press (AP)

AP covers alternative music,
media, and fashion.

Alternative Press
6516 Detroit Ave., ste 5
Cleveland, OH 44102
Phone: 216-631-1510
Fax: 216-631-1016

Audio-Gliphix

This publication covers
underground dance culture, hip-
hop, world beat, and Latin.

Audio-Gliphix
52123 Ninth and Market Streets
Philadelphia, PA 19105
Phone: 215-748-2037
Fax: 215-748-4193

Ball Buster

Ball Buster covers all types of
hard music.

Ball Buster
P.O. Box 58369
Louisville, KY 40268
Phone: 502-995-3396
Fax: 502-995-3396

Blaze

Published ten times a year, *Blaze*

covers hip-hop music, art, and culture.

Blaze
215 Lexington Ave., sixth flr.
New York, NY 10016
Phone: 212-448-7300
Fax: 212-448-7377

Blue Suede News
This publication is dedicated to classic and emerging blues.

Blue Suede News
P.O. Box 25
Duvall, WA 98019
Phone: 425-788-2776

CMJ New Music Monthly
This monthly magazine covers an eclectic array of music genres and includes a CD of new artists in every issue. The publication has circulation of 110,000.

CMJ New Music Monthly
Customer Service
P.O. Box 57414
Boulder, CO 80321
Phone: 800-682-7644

Cool Beans
Cool Beans contains interviews with and reviews of punk and indie artists. The publication comes with a compilation CD.

Cool Beans
3181 Mission #113
San Francisco, CA 94110
Phone: 415-771-6288
Fax: 415-771-6288

Country Music
This publication is dedicated to new country.

Country Music
49 East Twenty-first St.,
eleventh flr.

New York, NY 10010
Phone: 212-260-7210

Creative Loafing
A free weekly alternative newspaper based in Atlanta, *Creative Loafing* contains an expansive music section.

Creative Loafing
P.O. Box 54223
Atlanta, GA 30312
Phone: 404-688-5623
Fax: 404-614-3599

Dirty Linen
Dirty Linen covers a wide array of genres including roots, world, and folk.

Dirty Linen
P.O. Box 66600
Baltimore, MD 21239
Phone: 410-583-7973
Fax: 410-337-6735

Discorder
This punk rock magazine is published by the University of British Columbia.

Discorder
University of British Columbia
c/o CiTR
6138 Sub Blvd. #223
BC, V6T 1Z1 Canada
Phone: 604-822-3017
Fax: 604-822-9364

Downbeat
Downbeat covers a variety of roots and improvisational music.

Downbeat
102 N. Haven Rd.
Elmhurst, IL 60126
Phone: 630-941-2030
Fax: 630-941-3210

Flagpole

A free weekly arts magazine based in Athens, *Flagpole* contains an expansive music section.

Flagpole Magazine
112 S. Foundry St.
Athens, GA 30601
Phone: 706-549-9523
Fax: 706-548-8981

HM

HM covers the hard edge of Christian music.

HM
6614 Bradley Dr.
Austin, TX 78723
Phone: 512-929-9279
Fax: 512-929-1950

Ink 19

Ink 19 covers breaking, local, and touring acts in Florida.

Ink 19
4048 W. Kennedy Blvd., #652
Tampa, FL 33609
Phone: 813-837-1834
Fax: 813-837-1809

Island Ear

This publication provides regional entertainment news for Long Island and New York City.

Island Ear
2-12 W. Park Ave., ste. 214
Long Beach, NY 11561
Phone: 516-889-6045
Fax: 516-889-5513

Jam

In addition to acting as a resource for amateur and professional musicians, *Jam* provides regional coverage of emerging and touring acts.

Jam
P.O. Box 151720
Altamonte Springs, FL 32751
Phone: 407-767-8377
Fax: 407-767-0533

Jazz Now

Jazz Now covers all types of jazz through interviews and reviews.

Jazz Now
3733 California St.
Oakland, CA 94619
Phone: 510-531-2839
Fax: 510-531-8875

JazzTimes

This publication is dedicated to traditional jazz.

JazzTimes
8737 Colesville Rd., fifth flr.
Silversprings, MD 99050
Phone: 301-588-4114
Fax: 301-588-5531

Jersey Beat

Published three times a year, *Jersey Beat* covers an eclectic mix of music.

Jersey Beat
418 Gregory Ave.
Weehawken, NJ 07087
Phone: 201-864-6054
Fax: 201-864-9054

Living Blues

Living Blues is a nonprofit publication published by the University of Mississippi.

Living Blues
University of Mississippi
P.O. Box 1848

391 Hill Hall
Mississippi 38677
Phone: 662-915-5742
Fax: 662-915-7842

Music Monthly

Music Monthly covers music in
the Baltimore and Washington,
D.C., areas.

Music Monthly
1144 York Rd.
Lutherville, MD 21093
Phone: 410-494-0566
Fax: 410-494-0565

Music Morsels

In addition to interviewing
industry professionals, this
monthly publication covers
breaking acts.

Music Morsels
P.O. Box 672216
Marietta, GA 30006
Phone: 770-850-9560
Fax: 770-850-9646

Music News

Music News covers local and
touring acts.

Music Paper

In addition to equipment
reviews, the *Music Paper* covers
local and emerging acts.

Music Paper
P.O. Box 5167
Bay Shore, NY 11706
Phone: 516-666-4892
Fax: 516-666-7445

No Depression

No Depression covers alternative
country and Americana.
No Depression

P.O. Box 31332
Seattle, WA 98103
Phone: 206-706-7342
Fax: 206-706-3143

Offbeat

This monthly publication covers
cajun, blues, zydeco, jazz, rock,
blues, and R&B. *Offbeat* also
concentrates on Louisiana fairs
and festivals.

Offbeat
421 Frenchmen St., ste. 200
New Orleans, LA 70116

Outburn

Outburn covers equipment and
post-alternative music.

Outburn
P.O. Box 3187
Thousand Oaks, CA 91359
Phone: 805-493-5861
Fax: 805-493-5609

Pulse

Published by Tower Records,
Pulse covers all genres of
music.

Pulse
2500 Del Monte St., bldg. C
West Sacramento, CA 95691
Phone: 916-373-2450
Fax: 916-373-2480

Puncture

Puncture covers an eclectic
variety of alternative music.

Puncture
4031 S.E. Seventy-third Ave.
P.O. Box 14806
Portland, OR 97293
Phone: 503-777-4611
Fax: 503-777-4627

Rap Pages

This monthly covers hip-hop music, culture, and fashion.

Rap Pages
8484 Wilshire Blvd., ste. 900
Beverly Hills, CA 90211
Phone: 323-651-5400
Fax: 323-651-0651

Real Blues

A bimonthly publication, *Real Blues* focuses on emerging and indie blues, zydeco, gospel, swing, soul, and R&B artists.

Real Blues
302-655 Herald St.
Victoria, B.C. V8W 3L6
Canada
Phone: 250-384-2088
Fax: 250-384-2088

Relix

This bimonthly covers all genres but specializes in psychedelia.

Relix
P.O. Box 94
Brooklyn, NY 11229
Phone: 718-285-0009
Fax: 718-692-4345

Request

Request covers an eclectic array of emerging genres and music trends.

Request Magazine
10400 Yellow Circle Dr.
Minnetonka, MN 55343
Phone: 612-937-8740
Fax: 612-931-8490

Rock City News

This biweekly publication covers the Los Angeles music scene.

Rock City News
7030 De Longpre Ave.
Los Angeles, CA 90028
Phone: 323-461-6600
Fax: 323-461-6622

Ska-tastrophe

This quarterly covers breaking and underground ska, rock-steady, dub, and reggae.

Ska-tastrophe
P.O. Box 2102
Winter Park, FL 32790
Phone: 407-894-2930
Fax: 407-894-7877

SLAMM

SLAMM is a monthly San Diego–based alternative and local music magazine.

SLAMM
3530 Camino Del Rio N., ste. 105
San Diego, CA 92108
Phone: 619-281-7526
Fax: 619-281-5273

Rock N Roll Reporter

A monthly publication, *Rock N Roll Reporter* covers a wide variety of rock-related styles.

Rock N Roll Reporter
P.O. Box 575
MeKees Rocks, PA 15136
Phone: 412-771-1968
Fax: 412-771-1974

Rockrgrl

This quarterly publication is dedicated to covering, promoting, and educating female rock musicians.

Rockrgrl
7683 S.E. Twenty-seventh St., #317

Mercer Island, WA 98040
Phone: 206-230-4280
Fax: 206-230-4288

Seconds

This bimonthly publications specializes in interviewing artists from all genres.

Seconds
24 Fifth Ave., ste. 405
New York, NY 10011
Phone: 212-260-0481
Fax: 212-260-0440

The Source

The Source covers hip-hop music, art, and culture.

The Source
215 Park Ave. S., eleventh flr.
New York, NY 10001
Phone: 212-253-3700
Fax: 212-253-9344

The Stranger

The Stranger covers Seattle alternative lifestyles, arts, and culture.

The Stranger
P.O. Box 1225
1122 East Pike
Seattle, WA 98122
Phone: 206-212-7101
Fax: 206-323-7203

Vibe

Vibe covers an eclectic array of urban music including reggae, rap, gospel, jazz, and R&B.

Vibe
215 Lexington Ave., sixth flr.
New York, NY 10016
Phone: 212-448-7300
Fax: 212-448-7400

RADIO STATIONS

Alabama

WEGL

Format: eclectic

WEGL
c/o Auburn University
116 Foy Union
Auburn, AL 36849
Phone: 334-844-4114
Fax: 334-844-4114

WVUA

Format: eclectic, primarily college rock and indie

WVUA
P.O. Box 870152
Tuscaloosa, AL 35487
Phone: 205-348-6461
Fax: 205-348-0375

Alaska

KBBI

Format: public radio and eclectic music

KBBI
3913 Kachemak Way
Homer, AK 99603
Phone: 907-235-7721
Fax: 907-235-2357

KCHU

Format: eclectic

KCHU
P.O. Box 467
Valdez, AK 99686
Phone: 907-835-4665
Fax: 907-835-2847

KNOM

Format: Christian

KNOM
P.O. Box 988
Nome, AK 99762
Phone: 907-443-5221
Fax: 907-443-5757

KRUA
Format: contact program director

KRUA
University of Alaska
Anchorage, AK
Phone: 907-786-6802

Arizona

KAMP
Format: eclectic

KAMP Student Radio
University of Arizona
Tucson, AZ 85702
Phone: 520-621-8173
Fax: 520-626-8303

KASC
Format: eclectic, mostly
alternative

KASR
Arizona State University
Walter Cronkite School of
Journalism
Stauffer Hall
Tempe, AZ 85281
Phone: 480-965-4160
Fax: 480-727-6413

Arkansas

KHDX
Format: contact program director

KHDX
c/o Hendrix College
1600 Washington Ave.
Conway, AR 72032
Phone: 501-450-1339

KLRC
Format: Christian

KLRC
c/o John Brown University
2000 W. University St
Fayetteville, AR 72703
Phone: 501-771-9000

KXRJ
Format: alternative and eclectic

KXRJ
c/o ATU
Hwy. 7
Russellville, AR 72801
Phone: 501-964-0806
Fax: 501-964-0806

California

KALX
Format: eclectic

KALX
University of California
26 Barrows Hall #5650
Berkley, CA 94720
Phone: 510-642-1111

KCR
Format: eclectic

KCR
San Diego State University
5500 Campanile Dr.
San Diego, CA 92231
Phone: 619-594-7014

KCSF
Format: contact program director

KCSF
City College of San Francisco
50 Phelan Ave
San Francisco, CA 94112
Phone: 415-239-3444

KCSS
    Format: contact program director

    KCSS
    801 Buena Vista
    Turlock, CA 95382
    Phone: 209-667-3378

KFSR
    Format: eclectic

    KFSR
    California State University
    5201 N. Maple
    MS #119
    Fresno, CA 93740
    Phone: 559-278-2598

KGCR
    Format: contact program director

    KGCR
    Grosmont College
    El Cajon, CA 92020
    Phone: 619-465-1700

KGUR
    Format: contact program director

    KGUR
    Cuerta College
    San Luis, CA 93407
    Phone: 805-546-3191

KGWC
    Format: eclectic

    KGWC
    15744 Golden West St.
    Huntington Beach, CA 92647
    Phone: 714-895-8261

KHSU
    Format: contact program director

    KHSU
    Humbolt State University
    1 Horpst St.

Arcata, CA 95521
Phone: 707-826-6086

KJCC
    Format: contact program director

    KJCC
    c/o San Jose City College
    2100 Moore Park Ave.
    San Jose, CA 95128
    Phone: 408-298-2181

KKSM
    Format: contact program director

    Palomar College
    1140 W. Mission Rd.
    San Marcos, CA 92069
    Phone: 619-744-1150

KLA
    Format: eclectic

    KLA
    c/o UCLA
    2400 Ackerman Union
    Los Angeles, CA 90024
    Phone: 310-825-9105

KLBC
    Format: contact program director

    KLBC
    Long Beach City College
    4901 E. Carson St.
    Long Beach, CA 90808
    Phone: 562-420-4300

KMUD
    Format: eclectic

    KMUD
    P.O. Box 135
    Redway, CA 95560
    Phone: 707-923-2513
    Fax: 707-923-2501

KNAB
    Format: contact program director

KNAB
Chapman University
One University Dr.
Orange, CA 92866
Phone: 714-744-7020

KPFA

Format: eclectic

1929 Martin Luther King Jr.
Way
Berkeley, CA 94704
Phone: 510-848-6767
Fax: 510-848-3812

KRFH

Format: eclectic

KRFH
c/o Department of Journalism
Humbolt State University
Arcata, CA 95521
Phone: 707-826-3257
Fax: 707-826-4770

KSAK

Format: eclectic

KSAK
c/o Mt. San Antonio College
1100 N. Grand Ave.
Walnut, CA 98179
Phone: 909-594-5611,
ext. 4696
Fax: 909-468-3940

KSCB

Format: eclectic

KSCB
P.O. Box 13401
Santa Barbara, CA 93107
Phone: 805-893-3757

KSCR

Format: eclectic

KSCR
404 Student Union
Los Angeles, CA 90089
Phone: 213-740-1486
Fax: 213-740-1853

KSFS

Format: eclectic

KSFS
c/o San Francisco State
University
1600 Haloway Ave.
San Francisco, CA 94132
Phone: 415-338-2428
Fax: 415-338-6896

KSJS

Format: eclectic

KSJS
San Jose State University
Hugh Gillis Hall #132
2100 Moor Park Ave.
San Jose, CA 95192
Phone: 408-298-2181
Fax: 408-287-7222

KSPB

Format: eclectic

KSPB
Stevenson, the Upper School
3152 Forest Lake Rd.
Pebble Beach, CA 93953
Phone: 831-625-5078
Fax: 831-625-5208

KSPC

Format: eclectic

KSPC
Pomana College
Thatcher Music Bldg.
340 N. College Ave.
Claremont, CA 91711
Phone: 909-621-8157
Fax: 909-607-1259

KSRH

Format: contact program
director

KSRH
185 Mission Ave.
San Rafael, CA 94901
Phone: 415-457-5314

KSSB

Format: contact program director

KSSB
California State University
5500 University Pkwy.
San Bernardino, CA 92407
Phone: 909-880-5772

KSSU

Format: eclectic

KSSU
c/o ASI
6000 J St.
Sacramento, CA 95819
Phone: 916-278-5882
Fax: 916-278-6278

KSTD

Format: eclectic

KSTD
San Diego State University
San Diego, CA 92182
Phone: 619-594-7014

KSUH

Format: eclectic

KSUH
California State University
Hayward
25800 Corlos Bee Blvd.
Hayward, CA 94542
Phone: 510-885-3588

KSUN

Format: eclectic

KSUN
Sonoma State University
1801 E. Cotat's Ave.
Rohnert Park, CA 94928
Phone: 707-664-2621

KUCR

Format: contact program director

University of California at
Riverside
Riverside, CA 92521
Phone: 909-787-3838
Fax: 909-787-3240

KULV

Format: contact program director

KULV
University of La Verne
1950 Third St.
La Verne, CA 91750
Phone: 909-596-1696

KUSF

Format: eclectic

KUSF
University of San Francisco
2130 Fulton St.

San Francisco, CA 94117
Phone: 415-386-KUSF

KWTR
Format: contact program director

KWTR
Whittier College
13406 E. Philadelphia
P.O. Box 634
Whittier, CA 90601
Phone: 562-907-4992

KXLU
Format: eclectic

KXLU
Loyola Marymount University
7900 Loyola Blvd.
Los Angeles, CA 90045
Phone: 310-338-KXLU

KYDS
Format: eclectic

KYDS
El Camino High School
4300 El Camino Ave.
Sacramento, CA 95821
Phone: 916-456-5199

Colorado

KCSU
Format: eclectic

KCSU
Colorado State University
Fort Collins, CO 80523
Phone: 970-491-1695

KDUR
Format: contact program director

KDUR
Fort Lewis College
100 Rim Dr.

Duragno, CO 81301
Phone: 303-247-7288

KEPC
Format: alternative

KEPC
5675 S. Academy Blvd.
Colorado Springs, CO 80906
Phone: 800-456-6847, ext. 7849
Fax: 719-540-7487

KGNU
Format: eclectic

KGNU
P.O. Box 885
Boulder, CO 80306
Phone: 303-449-4885

KRCX
Format: eclectic

KRCX
Regis University
3333 Regis Blvd
Denver, CO 80221
Phone: 303-964-5392

KVCU
Format: eclectic

KVCU
c/o University of Colorado
Campus Box 207
Boulder, CO 80309
Phone: 303-492-5031

Delaware

WVUD
Format: alternative

WVUD
Perkins Student Center
University of Delaware
Newark, DE 19716

Phone: 302-831-2701
Fax: 302-831-1399

Florida

WPRK
Format: contact program director

WPRK
1000 Holt Avenue #2745
Winter Park, FL 32789
Phone: 407-646-2446

WBUL
Format: contact program director

WBUL
University of South Florida
4202 E. Fowler Ave.
Ctr 2487
Tampa, FL 33602
Phone: 813-974-4906

WDGR
Format: contact program
director

WDGR
Miami-Dade Community Col.
Kendall Campus
11011 SW 104th St
Miami FL 33176

WMNF
Format: eclectic

WMNF
1210 E. Martin Luther King Jr.
Blvd.
Tampa, FL 33603
Phone: 813-238-8001
Fax: 813-238-1802

WUFI
Format: contact program
director

WUFI
c/o Florida International
University
Miami, FL 33265
Phone: 305-348-3071

WVUM
Format: alternative

WVUM
P.O. Box 248191
Coral Gable, FL 33124
Phone: 305-284-3131
Fax: 305-284-3132

District of Columbia

WGTB
Format: contact program director

WGTB
Georgetown University
432 Leavey Center
Washington, D.C. 20057
Phone: 202-687-3702

WRCW
Format: contact program director

WRCW
George Washington University
800 21st St. NW #602
Washington, D.C. 20052
Phone: 202-994-7314

Georgia

WGHR
Format: contact program director

WGHR
1100 S. Marietta Pkwy.
Marietta, GA 30068
Phone: 770-528-7354

WMRE
Format: eclectic

WMRE
Emory University
Drawer W
Atlanta, GA 30322
Phone: 404-727-9672
Fax: 404-727-WMRE

WOTA
Format: contact program director

WOTA
DeKalb College
555 N. Indian Creek Dr.
Clarkston, GA 30021
Phone: 404-299-4113

WPLH
Format: eclectic

WPLH
ABAC Box 36
Tifton, GA 31794
Phone: 912-386-7158
Fax: 912-386-7158

WRAS
Format: eclectic

WRAS
c/o Georgia State University
Rm. 226 University Center
Atlanta, GA 30303
Phone: 404-651-2240
Fax: 404-651-1705

WUOG
Format: contact program director

WUOG
University of Georgia
Box 2065 Tate Center
Athens, GA 30602
Phone: 706-542-8466

WVGS
Format: contact program director

WVGS
Georgia Southern University
Statesborough, GA 30460
Phone: 912-681-5507

WVVS
Format: contact program director

WVVS
Valdosta State University
1500 N. Patterson St.
Valdosta, GA 31698
Phone: 912-333-7313

Idaho

KUOI
Format: contact program director

KUOI
University of Idaho
Student Union
Campus Box 444272
Moscow, ID 83844
Phone: 208-885-6433

Illinois

WARG
Format: contact program director

WARG
Summit High School
7329 W. Sixty-third St.
Summit, IL, 60501
Phone: 708-458-9274

WAUG
Format: contact program director

WAUG
Augustana College
639 Thirty-eighth St.

Rock Island, IL 61201
Phone: 309-734-7513

WCRX
Format: contact program
director

WCRX
Columbia College
33 East Congress
Chicago, IL 60605
Phone: 312-663-1693

WDGC
Format: contact program director

WDGC
Downers Grove High School
5121 Main St.
Downers Grove, IL 60515
Phone: 630-271-6514

WEFT
Format: contact program director

WEFT
113 N. Market
Champaign, IL 61820
Phone: 217-359-9338

WEIU
Format: eclectic

WEIU
Radio and TV Center, rm. 139
Charleston, IL 61920
Phone: 217-581-7371

WESN
Format: contact program director

WESN
Illinois Wesleyon University
P.O. Box 2900
Bloomington, IL 61702
Phone: 309-556-2638

WHPK
Format: rap and rock

WHPK
University of Chicago
Reynolds Club
5706 S. University Ave
Chicago, IL 60637
Phone: 773-702-8289
Fax: 773-834-1488

WIDB
Format: eclectic

WIDB
c/o SIUC
Student Center, fourth flr.
Carbondale, IL 62901
Phone: 618-536-2361
Fax: 618-453-5488

WIUS
Format: alternative rock

WIUS
Western Illinois University
315 Sallee Hall
1 University Circle
Macomb, IL 61455
Phone: 309-298-3217
Fax: 309-298-2829

WJMU
Format: alternative, world, and
R&B

WJMU
1184 W. Main St.
Decatur, IL 62522
Phone: 217-424-6377

WKDI
Format: eclectic

WKDI
c/o Northern Illinois University
801 N. First St.

Dekalb, IL 60115
Phone: 815-753-1278

WLCA

Format: alternative

WLCA
5800 Godfrey Rd.
Godfrey, IL 62034
Phone: 618-466-8936

WLUW

Format: indie and alternative

WLUW
820 N. Michigan Ave.
Chicago, IL 60611
Phone: 312-915-6558
Fax: 312-915-7095

WLTL

Format: contact program director

WLTL
LaGrange Lyons Township High
School
100 S. Brainad
La Grange, IL 60525
Phone: 708-482-9285

WMCR

Format: contact program director

WMCR
c/o Monmouth College
700 E. Broadway
Monmouth, IL 61462
Phone: 309-457-2107

WMXM

Format: contact program director

WMXM
c/o Lake Forest College
555 N. Sheridan Rd.
Chicago, IL 60045
Phone: 847-735-5220

WNUR

Format: eclectic

WNUR
Northwestern University
1905 Sheridan Rd.
Evanston, IL 60208
Phone: 847-491-7102

WONU

Format: Christian

WONU
P. O. Box 888 River Rd.
Kankakee, IL 60901
Phone: 800-987-WONU

WOUI

Format: contact program director

WOUI
Olivet Nazarene University
One University Ave.
Bourbonnais, IL 60914
Phone: 312-576-3087

WPCD

Format: eclectic; mostly rap and
rock

WPCD
c/o Parkland College
2400 W. Bradley Ave.
Champaign, IL 61821
Phone: 217-373-3790
Fax: 217-373-3899

WRRG

Format: indie rock and eclectic

WRRG
2000 Fifth Ave.
River Grove, IL 60171
Phone: 708-583-3110
Fax: 708-583-3120

WUIC

Format: contact program director

WUIC
University of Chicago
700 S. Halsted St. #17
Chicago, IL 60607
Phone: 312-355-8514

WVJC
Format: contact program director

WVJC
Wabash Valley College
2200 College Drive
Mt. Carmel, IL 62863
Phone: 618-262-8989

WVKC
Format: eclectic

WVKC
P.O. Box 254
Knox College
2 East South St.
Galesburg, IL 61401
Phone: 309-341-7441
Fax: 309-341-7090

WZND
Format: urban and rock

WZND
Campus Box 4481
Normal, IL 61790
Phone: 309-438-5491

Indiana

WBKE
Format: contact program director

WBKE
Manchester College
Box 85
College Ave. North
North Manchester, IN 46962
Phone: 219-982-5424

WEAX
Format: contact program director

WEAX
Tri-State University
1 University Avenue
Angola, IN 46703
Phone: 219-665-7310

WFCI
Format: contact program director

WFCI
Franklin College
501 E. Monroe St.
Franklin, IN 46131
Phone: 317-738-8205

WFHB
Format: eclectic

WFHB
108 W. Fourth St.
Bloomingdale, IN 47402
Phone: 812-323-1200
Fax: 812-323-0320

WHAR
Format: contact program director

WHAR
Martin University
2171 Avondale Place
Indianapolis, IN 46218
Phone: 317-510-4713

WIUS
Format: eclectic

WIUS
Indiana University
815 E. Eighth St.
Bloomingdale, IN 47408
Phone: 812-744-7862

WSND
Format: contact program director

WSND
Notre Dame
315 LaFortune Student Center

South Bend, IN 46556
Phone: 219-631-4068

WSWI
Format: modern rock (weeks) and
eclectic (weekends)

WSWI
8600 University Blvd.
Evansville, IN 47712
Phone: 812-465-1665
Fax: 812-465-1665

WUEV
Format: eclectic

WUEV
University of Evansville
1800 Lincoln Ave.
Evansville, IN 47722
Phone: 812-479-2022

Iowa

KDIC
Format: eclectic

KDIC
Grinnell College
Box V4
Grinnelle, IA 50112
Phone: 515-269-3335

KGRK
Format: eclectic

KGRK
University of Northern Iowa
Lower Level Maucker Union
Cedar Falls, IA 50614
Phone: 319-273-6935
Fax: 319-273-2991

KIGC
Format: eclectic

KIGC
201 Trueblood Ave.

Oskaloosa, IA 52977
Phone: 515-673-1095

KLCR
Format: Contact program director

KLCR
Loras College
1450 Alta Vista
Dubuque, IA 52004
Phone: 319-588-7172

KRNL
Format: contact program director

KRNL
810 Commons Circle
Mt. Vernon, IA 52314
Phone: 319-895-4431

KRUI
Format: eclectic

KRUI
University of Iowa
Iowa City, IA 52242
Phone: 319-335-9525

KURE
Format: eclectic

KURE
Iowa State University
1199 Friley
Ames, IA 50012
Phone: 515-294-4332

Kansas

KANZ
Format: eclectic/NPR

KANZ
210 N. Seventh St.
Garden City, KS 67846
Phone: 316-275-7444
Fax: 316-275-7496

KJHK

Format: eclectic

KJHK
University of Kansas
2051 Dole Center
Lawrence, KS 66045
Phone: 785-864-4745

Kentucky

WMKY

Format: classical

WMKY
Morehead State University
UPO Box 903
Morehead, KY 40351
Phone: 606-783-2001
Fax: 606-783-2335

WNKV

Format: contact program director

WNKV
Northern Kentucky University
Nunn Drive
Highland Heights, KY 41099
Phone: 606-572-7897

WRFL

Format: contact program director

WRFL
Purdue University
Shreve Hall
West Lafayette IN 47907
Phone: 606-257-1557

WWHR

Format: alternative rock

Western Kentucky University
1 Big Red Way
Bowling Green, KY 42101
Phone: 270-745-5439

Louisiana

KLPI

Format: eclectic

KLPI
Louisiana Tech University
P.O. Box 3178
Ruston, LA 71272
Phone: 318-257-4852

KLSU

Format: eclectic

KLSU
Louisiana State University
B-39 Hodges Hall
Baton Rouge, LA 70803
Phone: 225-388-4620

KNSU

Format: new rock

KNSU
P.O. Box 2664
Thibodaux, LA 70310
Phone: 504-448-4446
Fax: 504-449-7106

KNWD

Format: eclectic

KNWD
NSU Box 3038
Natchitoches, LA 71497
Phone: 318-357-4180

KSCL

Format: contact program director

KSCL
Centenary College
2911 Centenary Blvd.
Shreveport, LA 71134
Phone: 318-869-2596

KXUL

Format: new rock

KXUL
University of Louisiana at
Monroe
130 Stubbs Hall
ULM
Monroe, LA 71209
Phone: 318-342-5658

WTUL

Format: eclectic

WTUL
Tulane University Center
New Orleans, LA 70118
Phone: 504-865-5887

Maine

WMEB

Format: contact program director

WMEB
University of Maine
Orono, ME 04469
Phone: 207-581-4341

WMHB

Format: eclectic

WMHB
Colby College
4000 Mayflower Hill
Waterville, ME 04901
Phone: 207-872-3686
Fax: 207-872-3785

WMPG

Format: eclectic

WMPG
University of Southern Main
96 Falmouth St.
Portland, ME 04101
Phone: 207-780-4976

WRBC

Format: eclectic

WRBC
Bates College
Lewiston, ME 04240
Phone: 207-777-7532

WSJB

Format: contact program
director

WSJB
Saint Joseph's College
278 Whitas Bridge Rd.
Standish, ME 04084
Phone: 207-893-7752

WUMF

Format: eclectic

WUMF
5 South St.
Farmington, ME 04938
Phone: 207-778-7352
Fax: 207-778-8190

Maryland

WHSR

Format: eclectic

WHSR
Johns Hopkins University
Mattin Center
3400 N. Charles St.
Baltimore, MD 21218
Phone: 410-516-3884

WMUC

Format: eclectic

WMUC Radio
University of Maryland
3130 S. Campus Dining Hall

College Park, MD 20742
Phone: 301-314-7868
Fax: 301-314-7879

WROC

Format: contact program director

WROC
Montgomery College
51 Mannakee St.
Rockville, MD 20850
Phone: 301-251-7178

WSUR

Format: alternative rock, hip-hop, and jazz

WSUR
Salisbury State University
P.O. Box 3064
Salisbury, MD 21801
Phone: 410-543-6195

WTMD

Format: smooth jazz

WTMD Radio
Townson University
8000 York Rd.
Townson, MD 21252
Phone: 410-830-8937
Fax: 410-830-2609

Massachusetts

WAMH

Format: eclectic

WAMH
Amherst College
Campus Center
Amherst, MA 01002
Phone: 413-542-2224

WBIM

Format: eclectic

WBIM
109 Campus Center
Bridgewater State College
Bridgewater, MA 02325
Phone: 508-697-1366
Fax: 508-531-1786

WCFM

Format: eclectic

WCFM
Baxter Hall
Williamstown, MA 01276
Phone: 413-597-2373
Fax: 413-597-2259

WDJM

Format: contact program director

WDJM
Framingham State College
Student Center
Framingham, MA 01702
Phone: 508-626-4623

WERS

Format: eclectic

WERS
Emerson College
120 Boylston St.
Boston, MA 02116
Phone: 617-578-8890
Fax: 617-824-8804

WJJW

Format: contact program director

WJJW
Massachusetts College
of Liberal Arts

375 Church St.
North Adams, MA 01247
Phone: 413-662-5405

WKKL
Format: eclectic

WKKL
Cape Cod Community College
Rte. 132
West Barnstable, MA 02668
Phone: 508-362-2131, ext. 4030
Fax: 508-375-4064

WMBR
Format: eclectic

WMBR
3 Ames St.
Cambridge, MA 02142
Phone: 617-253-4000
Fax: 617-232-1384

WMCI
Format: eclectic

WMCI
Massasoit Community College
1 Massasoit Blvd.
Brockton, MA 02402
Phone: 508-588-9100, ext. 1989

WMFO
Format: eclectic

WMFO
P.O. Box 65
Medford, MA 02153
Phone: 617-625-0800
Fax: 617-625-6072

WMLN
Format: contact program
director

WMLN
Mount Holyoke College
50 College St.

Milton, MA 01075
Phone: 617-333-2368

WMUA
Format: eclectic

WMUA
105 Campus Center
University of Massachusetts
Amherst, MA 01003
Phone: 413-545-8276

WMWM
Format: eclectic

WMWM
352 Lafayette St.
Salem, MA 01970
Phone: 978-745-9401
Fax: 978-741-9433

WNEK
Format: contact program
director

WNEK
Western New England College
1215 Wilbraham Rd.
Springfield, MA 01119
Phone: 413-782-1582

WOZQ
Format: contact program director

WOZQ
Davis Center
Smith College
Northampton, MA 01063
Phone: 413-585-4977

WRBB
Format: eclectic

WRBB
360 Huntington Ave #174
Boston, MA 02115
Phone: 617-373-4339

WRSI
Format: contact program director

WRSI
100 Main St.
Greenfield, MA 01060
Phone: 413-774-2321

WSHL
Format: contact program director

WSHL
Stonehill College
320 Washington St.
North Easton, MA 02357
Phone: 508-238-2612

WSKB
Format: modern rock and
eclectic

WSKB
Westfield St. College
Ely Building
Westfield, MA 01086
Phone: 413-572-5427
Fax: 413-572-5262

WSMU
Format: alternative and
eclectic

WSMU Radio
University of Massachussetts—
Dartmouth
Old Westport Rd.
North Dartmouth, MA 02747
Phone: 508-999-8149
Fax: 508-999-8173

WTBU
Format: eclectic

WTBU
Boston University
640 Commonwealth Ave.
Boston, MA 02215
Phone: 617-373-4339

WTCC
Format: eclectic

WTCC
1 Armoury Square
Springfield, MA 01105
Phone: 413-781-6628
Fax: 413-781-3747

WWPI
Format: eclectic

WWPI
100 Institute Rd.
Worcester, MA 01609
Phone: 508-831-5956

Michigan

CJAM
Format: eclectic

CJAM
University of Windsor
P.O. Box 33830
Detroit, MI 48232
Phone: 519-971-3606
Fax: 519-971-3605

WAQU
Format: contact program director

WAQU
Aquinas College
Wege Student Center
Grand Rapids, MI 49506
Phone: 616-453-8281

WCAL
Format: contact program director

WCAL
1607 Robinson Rd. S.E.
Grand Rapids, MI 49506
Phone: 616-957-8546

WCBN
Format: eclectic

WCBN
University of Michigan
530 Student Services Bldg.
Ann Arbor, MI 48109
Phone: 734-763-3501

WCKS

Format: contact program director

WCKS
104 Commons Bldg.
GBSU
Allendale, MI 49401
Phone: 616-895-2877

WDBM

Format: alternative and AAA

WDBM
G-4 Holden Hall
East Lansing, MI 48825
Phone: 517-353-4414
Fax: 571-355-6552

WDET

Format: eclectic

WDET
4600 Cass Ave.
Detroit, MI 48201
Phone: 313-577-4146
Fax: 313-577-1300

WHFR

Format: contact program director

WHFR
5101 Evergreen Rd.
Dearborn, MI 48128
Phone: 313-845-9676

WIDR

Format: contact program director

WIDR
Western Michigan University
1511 Faunce Student Service
Bldg.

Kalamazoo, MI 49008
Phone: 616-387-6396

WLBN

Format: contact program director

WLBN
Albion College
611 E. Porter St.
Albion, MI 49224
Phone: 517-629-0528

WMHW

Format: contact program director

WMHW
Central Michigan University
Mt. Pleasant, MI 48859
Phone: 517-774-7287

WMNC

Format: eclectic

WMNC
1701 E. Front St.
Traverse City, MI 49686
Phone: 231-922-1091

WMTU

Format: eclectic

WMTU
1703 Townsend Dr.
Houghton, MI 49931
Phone: 906-487-2333
Fax: 906-487-3016

WQAC

Format: contact program director

WQAC
Alma College
614 W. Superior St.
Alma, MI 48801
Phone: 517-463-7095

WSDP

Format: contact program director

WSDP
46181 Joy Rd.
Canton, MI 48187
Phone: 313-416-7732

WTHS
Format: alternative and
eclectic

WTHS
DeWitt Student Center
Hope College
Holland, MI 49423
Phone: 616-395-7878
Fax: 616-395-7958

WUPX
Format: eclectic

WUPX
Northern Michigan University
1204 University Center
Marquette, MI 49855
Phone: 906-227-1844
Fax: 906-277-2344

Minnesota

KFAI
Format: eclectic

KFAI
1808 Riverside Ave.
Minneapolis, MN 55454
Phone: 612-341-3144
Fax: 612-341-4281

KJNB
Format: eclectic

KJNB
St. John's University
P.O. Box 1255
Minneapolis, MN 56321
Phone: 320-363-3380
Fax: 320-363-3492

KMSC
Format: eclectic

KMSC
Minnesota State University—
Moorehead
P.O. Box 356
Owens Hall
Mankato, MN 56560
Phone: 218-236-2116
Fax: 218-236-2116

KMSU
Format: rock and eclectic

KMSU
Minnesota State University
AF205
Mankato, MN 56560
Phone: 507-389-5678
Fax: 507-389-1705

KORD
Format: alternative and techno

KORD
Concordia College
P.O. Box 3007
Moorhead, MN 56562
Phone: 218-299-3028

KSTO
Format: eclectic

KSTO
1500 St. Olof Ave.
Northfield, MN 55057
Phone: 507-646-3603
Fax: 507-646-3957

KUMM
Format: eclectic

KUMM
600 E. Fourth St.
Morris, MN 56267
Phone: 320-589-6076
Fax: 320-589-6075

KUOM
Format: eclectic

KUOM
330 Twenty-first Ave. S.
Minneapolis, MN 55455
Phone: 800-626-4770
Fax: 612-625-2112

KVSC
Format: eclectic

KVSC
St. Cloud State University
27 Stewart Hall
St. Cloud, MN 56301
Phone: 320-255-3126

WMCM
Format: eclectic

WMCM
P.O. Box 356
Owens Hall
Minnesota State University—
Moorehead
Mankato, MN 56560
Phone: 651-696-6312
Fax: 651-696-6312

Mississippi

WUSM
Format: eclectic

WUSM
Southern Station Box 10045
Hattiesburg, MS 39406
Phone: 601-266-4287
Fax: 601-266-4288

Missouri

KCFV
Format: alternative

KCFV
3400 Perschall Rd.
St. Louis, MO 63135
Phone: 314-595-4478/-4217

KCOU
Format: eclectic

KCOU
University of Missouri
101F Pershing Hall
Columbia, MO 65201
Phone: 573-882-7820

KGSP
Format: contact program director

KGSP
Park University
Parkville, MO 64152
Phone: 816-741-2000, ext. 6325

KMNR
Format: eclectic

KMNR
113 E. University Center W.
1870 Minor Circle
Rolla, MO 65409
Phone: 573-341-4272
Fax: 573-341-6021

KPNT
Format: eclectic

KPNT
1215 Cole St.
St. Louis, MO 63106
Phone: 314-231-1057

KTRM
Format: eclectic

KTRM
Sherman State University
Dept. of Language and
Literature—SUB
Kirksville, MO 63501
Phone: 660-785-4506
Fax: 660-785-7261

KWUR
Format: eclectic

KWUR
Washington University
Campus Box 1205
1 Brookings Dr.
St. Louis, MO 63105
Phone: 314-935-5952
Fax: 314-935-5699

Montana

KBGA
Format: eclectic

KBGA
University of Montana
Missoula, MT 59812
Phone: 406-243-5715

KGLT
Format: eclectic

KGLT
Montana State University
P.O. Box 173350
Bozeman, MT 59717
Phone: 406-994-6483

KMSM
Format: contact program director

KMSM
Montana Tech
1300 W. Park St., Rm. 117
Butte, MT 59701
Phone: 406-496-4391

Nebraska

KDCV
Format: contact program director

KDCV
Dana College
2848 College Drive
Blair, NE 68008
Phone: 402-426-7205

KFKX
Format: contact program director

KFKX
Hastings College
800 N. Turner
Hastings, NE 68901
Phone: 402-461-7460

KLPR
Format: contact program director

KLPR
University of Nebraska at
Kearney
905 W. Twenty-fifth St.
Kearney, NE 68849
Phone: 308-865-8216

KRNU
Format: alternative

KRNU
206 Avery Hall
University of Nebraska
Lincoln, NE 68588
Phone: 402-472-3054
Fax: 402-472-8403

KWSC
Format: contact program director

KWSC
Wayne State College
1111 Main St.
Wayne, NE 68787
Phone: 402-375-7536

KZUM
Format: eclectic

KZUM
941 O St.
Lincoln, NE 68508
Phone: 402-474-5086
Fax: 402-474-5091

Nevada

KEDP
Format: eclectic

KEDP
4505 Maryland Pkwy.
Las Vegas, NV 89154
Phone: 702-895-3877
Fax: 702-895-0983

New Hampshire

WDCR
Format: eclectic

WDCR
P.O. Box 957
Hanover, NH 03755
Phone: 603-646-3932
Fax: 603-643-7655

WFPR
Format: contact program director

WFPR
Franklin Pierce College
20 College Rd.
Rindge, NH 03461
Phone: 603-899-4137

WKNH
Format: contact program director

WKNH
Keene State College
229 Main St.
Keene, NH 03435
Phone: 603-358-2420

WMAX
Format: contact program director

WMAX
400 Commercial St.
Manchester, NH 03101
Phone: 603-627-7999

WNEC
Format: eclectic

WNEC
Simon Center

Henniker, NH 03242
Phone: 603-428-6393
Fax: 603-428-2543

WUNH
Format: eclectic

WUNH
c/o University of New Hampshire
Memorial Union Building
Durham, NH 03824
Phone: 603-862-2541
Fax: 603-862-2543

New Jersey

WCUH
Format: eclectic

WCUH
Hunterdon Central Regional
High School
84 Rte. 31
Flemington, NJ 08822
Phone: 908-782-9595

WFDQ
Format: eclectic

WFDQ
Fairleigh Dickinson University
1000 River Rd.
Teaneck, NJ 07666
Phone: 201-692-2103

WGKR
Format: metal, urban, world, and
alternative

WGKR
New Jersey City University
2039 Kennedy Blvd.
Jersey City, NJ 07305
Phone: 201-200-3556

WGLS
Format: eclectic

WGLS
Rowan University
201 Mullica Hill Rd.
Glassboro, NJ 08028
Phone: 609-863-9457

WJSV

Format: contact program director

WJSV
Morristown High School
50 Early St.
Morristown, NJ 07960
Phone: 201-292-2186

WLFR

Format: contact program director

WLFR
Richard Stockton College
P.O. Box 195
Pomona, NJ 08240
Phone: 609-652-4780

WPRB

Format: contact program director

WPRB
P.O. Box 342
Princeton, NJ 08542
Phone: 609-258-3655
Fax: 609-258-1806

WRRC

Format: contact program director

WRRC
Rider University
2083 Lawrenceville Rd.
Lawrenceville, NJ 08648
Phone: 609-896-5369

WRSU

Format: eclectic

WRSU
126 College Ave.
New Brunswick, NJ 08903
Phone: 732-932-7800

WSOU

Format: rock

WSOU
400 S. Orange Ave.
South Orange, NJ 07079
Phone: 800-895-WSOU
Fax: 793-461-7593

WTSR

Format: eclectic

WTSR
The College of New Jersey
Kendall Hall
P.O. Box 7718
Ewing, NJ 08628
Phone: 609-771-2420

New Mexico

KRUX

Format: contact program director

KRUX
New Mexico State University
Las Cruces, NM
Phone: 505-646-4640
Fax: 505-646-8919

KUNM

Format: eclectic

KUNM
University of New Mexico
Oñate Hall
Albuquerque, NM 87131
Phone: 505-277-8022

KTEK

Format: eclectic

KTEK
New Mexico Tech
Socorro, NM 87801
Phone: 505-835-6013

New York

WAIH
Format: contact program director

WAIH
Suny Potsdam
44 Pierrepont Ave.
Potsdam, NY 13676
Phone: 315-267-2511

WARY
Format: contact program director

WARY
Westchester Community College
75 Grasslands Rd.
Valhalla, NY 10595
Phone: 914-785-6152

WBAU
Format: contact program director

WBAU
Adelphi University
Garden City, NY 11530
Phone: 516-877-6400

WBCR
Format: contact program director

WBCR
Brooklyn College
2900 Bedford Ave.
Brooklyn, NY 11210
Phone: 718-859-6314

WBMB
Format: rock and alternative

WBMB
17 Lexington Ave.

New York, NY 10010
Phone: 212-802-6760

WBSU
Format: eclectic

WBSU
SUNY—Brockport
Seymour Union
Brockport, NY 14420
Phone: 716-395-2580

WCDB
Format: eclectic

WCDB
SUNY—Albany
Campus Center 316
1400 Washington Ave.
Albany, NY 12222
Phone: 518-442-5262
Fax: 518-442-4366

WCEB
Format: eclectic

WCEB
Corning Community College
1 Academic Dr.
Corning, NY 14830
Phone: 607-962-9360
Fax: 607-962-9456

WCVM
Format: contact program director

WCVM
SUNY—Morrisville
020 Charlton Hall
Morrisville, NY 13408
Phone: 315-684-6358

WCWF
Format: eclectic

WCWF
115 McEwen Hall
SUNY—Fredonia

Fredonia, NY 14063
Phone: 716-673-3420
Fax: 716-673-3427

WDFH
Format: eclectic

WDFH
Dobbs Ferry, NY 10522
Phone: 914-693-3963
Call before sending demos

WDWN
Format: alternative and hip-hop

WDWN
197 Franklin St.
Auburn, NY 13021
Phone: 315-255-1743
Fax: 315-255-2690

WFCX
Format: contact program director

WFCX
St. John Fisher College
3690 East Ave.
Rochester, NY 14618
Phone: 716-385-8174

WFMU
Format: eclectic

WFMU
P.O. Box 5101
Hoboken, NJ 07030
Phone: 201-200-9362

WFNP
Format: contact program director

WFNP
SUNY—New Paltz
Sub 413
New Paltz, NY 12561
Phone: 914-257-3041

WGSU
Format: alternative rock

WGSU
Blake B-104
1 College Circle
Geneseo, NY 14454
Phone: 716-245-5486
Fax: 716-245-5240

WMPC
Format: contact program director

WMPC
Nassau Community College
1 Education Dr.
Garden City, NY 11530
Phone: 516-572-7438
Fax: 516-572-7783

WHRO
Format: eclectic

WHRO
Hartwick College
West St.
Oneonta, NY 13820
Phone: 607-431-4005

WHSE
Format: contact program director

WHSE
Smithtown High School
100 Central Rd.
Smithtown, NY 11787
Phone: 631-862-1534

WICR
Format: contact program director

WICR
Iona College
715 North Ave.
New Rochelle, NY 10801
Phone: 631-633-2369

WIRE
Format: contact program director

WIRE
Dowling College
Idle Hour Blvd.
Oakdale, NY 11769
Phone: 516-244-3027

WITR
Format: eclectic

WITR
32 Lomb Memorial Dr.
Rochester, NY 14623
Phone: 716-475-2000
Fax: 716-475-7988

WKCR
Format: jazz, classical, and avant garde

WKCR
Columbia University
New York, NY 10027
Phone: 212-854-5223
Fax: 212-854-9296

WONY
Format: contact program director

WONY
Oneonta, NY 13820
Call before sending demos
Phone: 607-436-2712

WPLT
Format: eclectic

WPLT
101 Broad St.
SUNY—Plattsburg
Plattsburg, NY 12901
Phone: 518-564-2727
Fax: 518-564-3994

WPNR
Format: eclectic

WPNR
1600 Burrstone Rd.
Utica, NY 13502
Phone: 315-792-3069
Fax: 315-792-3292

WPOB
Format: contact program director

WPOB
50 Kennedy Dr.
Plainview, NY 11803
Phone: 516-937-6375

WRCM
Format: eclectic

WRCM
Manhattan College Radio
Manhattan College Parkway
New York, NY 10471
Phone: 718-920-0444

WRHU
Format: eclectic

WRHU
Hofstra University, rm. 127
Hempstead, NY 11549
Phone: 516-463-5105

WRNU
Format: contact program director

WRNU
Niagra University
c/o Media Resources
Niagara, NY 14109
Phone: 716-286-8478

WRPI
Format: eclectic

WRPI
Rensselaer Polytechnic Institute
1 WRPI Plaza
Troy, NY 12180
Phone: 518-276-8648

WRPW

Format: contact program director

WRPW
Pace University
861 Bedford Rd.
Pleasantville, NY 10570
Phone: 914-773-3703

WRUB

Format: contact program director

WRUB
174 MSAC
Amherst, NY 14261
Phone: 716-645-3370

WRUC

Format: contact program director

WRUC
Union College
Reamer Campus Center, fourth flr.
Schenectady, NY 12308
Phone: 518-388-6154

WRUR

Format: contact program director

WRUR
University of Rochester
P.O. Box 277356
Rochester, NY 14627
Phone: 716-275-6400

WSBU

Format: modern rock

WSBU
St. Bonaventure University
P.O. Box Draw O
St. Bonaventure, NY 14778
Phone: 716-375-2307
Fax: 716-375-4008

WSIA

Format: eclectic

WSIA
2800 Victory Blvd.
Staten Island, NY 10314
Phone: 718-982-3057

WSPN

Format: contact program director

WSPN
Skidmore College
815 North Broadway
Saratoga Springs, NY 12866
Phone: 518-584-7378

WSUC

Format: alternative and industrial

WSUC
SUNY—Cortland
P.O. Box 2000
Cortland, NY 13045
Phone: 607-753-2963

WUSB

Format: eclectic

WUSB
SUNY—Stony Brook
Union Building
Stony Brook, NY 11794
Phone: 631-632-6501

WVBR

Format: contact program director

WVBR
957-B Mitchell St.
Ithaca, NY 14850
Phone: 607-273-4000
Fax: 607-273-4069

WVCR

Format: urban

WVCR
515 Louden Rd.
Loudonville, NY 12211
Phone: 518-783-2990

WVHC
Format: eclectic

WVHC
100 Reservoir
Herkimer, NY 13350
Phone: 315-866-0300, ext. 354

WVIC
Format: contact program director

WVIC
Ithaca College
Ithaca, NY 14850
Phone: 607-274-1040

WVKR
Format: eclectic

WVKR
P.O. Box 726
Marist College
Poughkeepsie, NY 12604
Phone: 914-437-5476

WYNO
Format: eclectic

WYNO
SUNY—Oswego
Oswego, NY 13126
Phone: 315-341-2101

North Carolina

WKNC
Format: eclectic

WKNC
P.O. Box 8607
Raleigh, NC 37695
Phone: 919-515-2401
Fax: 919-513-2693

WQFS
Format: contact program director

WQFS
5800 W. Friendly Ave.

Greensboro, NC 27410
Phone: 336-316-2352
Fax: 336-316-2949

WWIH
Format: contact program director

WWIH
High Point University
833 Montlieu Ave.
Campus Box 3071
High Point, NC 27262
Phone: 336-841-9634

WXDU
Format: eclectic

WXDU
P.O. Box 90689
Durham, NC 22708
Phone: 919-684-2957
Fax: 919-684-3260

WXYC
Format: eclectic

WXYC
University of North Carolina—
Chapel Hill
P.O. Box 51
Carolina Union
Chapel Hill, NC 27599
Phone: 919-962-7768

Ohio

ACRN
Format: contact program director

ACRN
Ohio University
9 South College St. #315
Athens, OH 45701
Phone: 740-593-4910

WBGU
Format: contact program director

WBGU
Bowling Green State University
West Hall
Bowling Green, OH 43403
Phone: 419-372-8657

WBWC
Format: alternative rock and
eclectic

WBWC
Baldwin-Wallace College
275 Eastland Rd.
Berea, OH 44017
Phone: 440-826-8525
Fax: 440-826-3426

WGXM
Format: eclectic

WGXM
300 College Park
Kennedy Union
Dayton, OH 45401
Phone:937-229-3058

WJCU
Format: contact program director

WJCU
John Carroll University
University Heights, OH 44118
Phone: 216-397-4437

WKCO
Format: contact program director

WKCO
Kenyon College
P.O. Box 312
Gambier, OH 43022
Phone: 614-427-5412

WKHR
Format: big band

WKHR
17425 Synder Rd.
Chagrin Falls, OH 44023

Phone: 440-543-9646
Fax: 440-543-9021

WMSR
Format: eclectic

WMSR
Miami University of Ohio
221 Williams Hall
Oxford, OH 45056
Phone: 513-529-1269

WOBC
Format: eclectic

WOBC
Oberlin College
319 Wilder Hall
135 W. Lorain St.
Oberlin, OH 44074
Phone: 440-775-8170

WOBN
Format: alternative rock

WOBN
Cawan Hall
Otterbein College
Westerville, OH 43081
Phone: 614-823-1557
Fax: 614-823-1996

WOXY
Format: eclectic

WOXY
5120 College Corner Pike
Oxford, OH 45056
Phone: 513-529-1269

WRDL
Format: contact program director

WRDL
Ashland University
401 College Ave.
Ashland, OH 44805
Phone: 419-289-5139

WVXU
Format: contact program director

WVXU
Xavier University
3800 Victory Pkwy.
Cincinnati, OH 45207
Phone: 513-731-9898
Fax: 513-745-1004

WWSU
Format: contact program director

WWSU
Wright State University
WO22 Student Union
Dayton, OH 45435
Phone: 937-873-5554

WYSO
Format: eclectic

WYSO
Antioch University
795 Livermore St.
Dayton, OH 45387
Phone: 937-767-6422

Oregon

KBOO
Format: alternative

KBOO
20 S.E. Eighth Ave.
Portland, OR 97214
Phone: 503-231-8032
Fax: 503-231-7145

KBVR
Format: eclectic

KBVR
210 Memorial Union East
Corvallis, OR 97331
Phone: 541-737-2008
Fax: 541-757-4545

KEOL
Format: eclectic

KEOL
Eastern Oregon University
One University Blvd.
La Grande, OR 97850
Phone: 503-962-3397

KLCC
Format: contact program director

KLCC
4000 East Thirtieth Ave.
Eugene, OR 97405
Phone: 503-768-7133

KPSU
Format: eclectic

KPSU
Portland State University
P.O. Box 751-SD
Portland, OR 97202
Phone: 503-725-5669

KWVA
Format: eclectic

KWVA
University of Oregon
P.O. Box 3157
Eugene, OR 97403
Phone: 541-346-4091

Pennsylvania

WCCB
Format: contact program director

WCCB
Clarion University
Clarion, PA 16214
Phone: 814-226-2717

WCUR
Format: contact program director

WCUR
West Chester University
237 Sykes Union
West Chester, PA 19383
Phone: 610-436-2414

WDCV

Format: contact program director

WDCV
Dickinson College
Carlisle, PA 17013
Phone: 717-245-1661

WDSR

Format: eclectic

WDSR
Duguesne University
SMC #2500
1345 Vickory St.
Pittsburgh, PA
Phone: 412-396-5773
Fax: 412-396-1661

WEHR

Format: contact program director

WEHR
104 Johnston Commons
University Park, PA 16802
Phone: 814-865-0897
Fax: 814-865-3252

WFNM

Format: contact program director

WFNM
Franklin and Marshall College
P.O. Box 3003
Lancaster, PA 17604
Phone: 717-291-4098

WFSE

Format: alternative, urban, and
eclectic

WFSE
Edinboro University
Edinboro, PA 16444
Phone: 814-732-2526
Fax: 814-732-2427

WKDU

Format: eclectic

WKDU
3210 Chestnut St.
Philadelphia, PA 19104
Phone: 215-895-5920

WLHU

Format: contact program director

WLHU
Lock Haven University
Robinson Hall
Lock Haven, PA 17745
Phone: 570-893-2523

WLVR

Format: contact program director

WLVR
Lehigh University
29 Trembly Drive
Bethlehem, PA 18015
Phone: 610-758-4187

WMCE
Format: classical

WMCE
Mercyhurst College
501 E. Thirty-eighth St.
Erie, PA 16546
Phone: 814-824-2261

WMUH
Format: contact program director

WMUH
Muhlenberg College
Box 2806

Allentown, PA 18104
Phone: 610-821-3239

WNTE
Format: eclectic

WNTE
P.O. Box 84
South Hall
Mansfield University
Mansfield, PA 16933
Phone: 570-662-4650

WPTC
Format: eclectic

WPTC
Penn College
1 College Ave.
Williamsport, PA 17701
Phone: 570-327-4778

WQHS
Format: eclectic

WQHS
University of Pennsylvania
3905 Spruce St.
Philadelphia, PA 19104
Phone: 215-898-9553

WQSU
Format: modern rock and
alternative

WQSU
Susquehanna University
514 University Ave.
Selinsgrove, PA 07870
Phone: 570-372-4100

WRCT
Format: eclectic

WRCT
Carnegie Mellon University
1 WRCT Plaza
5000 Forbes Ave.

Pittsburgh, PA 15213
Phone: 412-621-0728

WRKU
Format: contact program director

WRKU
Kutztown University
Kutztown, PA 19530
Phone: 610-683-4059

WSFX
Format: eclectic

WSFX
Luzerne County Community
College
1333 S. Prospect
Nanticoke, PA 18634
Phone: 717-821-0933

WSRN
Format: eclectic

WSRN
Swarthmore College
500 College Ave.
Swarthmore, PA 19081
Phone: 610-328-8340

WSYC
Format: eclectic

WSYC
Shippensberg University
Cumberland Union Building
Shippensberg, PA 17257
Phone: 717-532-6006

WUSR
Format: eclectic

WUSR
University of Scranton
Student Radio
Scranton, PA 08510
Phone: 570-941-7648
Fax: 570-941-4372

WWEC
Format: eclectic

WWEC
Elizabethtown College
1 Alpha Dr.
Elizabethtown, PA 17022
Phone: 717-361-1412

WXAC
Format: contact program director

WXAC
Albright College
Thirteenth and Bern Sts.
Reading, PA 19612
Phone: 610-921-7545

WXLV
Format: eclectic

WXLV
4525 Education Park Dr.
Schnecksville, PA 18078
Phone: 610-799-4141
Fax: 610-799-1571

WXVU
Format: eclectic

WXVU
Villanova University
210 Dougherty Hall
800 Lancaster Ave.
Villanova, PA 19085
Phone: 610-519-7200

WYBF
Format: contact program director

WYBF
Cabrini College
610 King of Prussia Rd.
Radnor, PA 19087
Phone: 610-902-8457

WZBT
Format: contact program director

WZBT
Gettysburg College
Box 435
Gettysburg, PA 17325
Phone: 717-337-6315

Rhode Island

WELH
Format: contact program director

WELH
Rhode Island College
600 Mount Pleasant Ave.
Student Union 309
Providence, RI 02908
Phone: 401-421-8100

WJMF
Format: contact program director

WJMF
Bryant College
1150 Douglas Pike
Smithfield, RI 02917
Phone: 401-232-6044
Fax: 401-232-6177

WXIN
Format: eclectic

WXIN
Rhode Island College
600 Mt. Pleasant Ave.
Student Union, rm. 309
Providence, RI 02908
Phone: 401-456-8288
Fax: 401-456-8541

South Carolina

WUSC
Format: eclectic

WUSC
1400 Green St.
Columbia, SC 29208
Phone: 803-576-WUSC

South Dakota

KBHU
Format: contact program director

KBHU
Black Hills State University
1200 University St. #9665
Spearfish, SD 57799
Phone: 605-642-6737

KSDJ
Format: alternative rock

KSDJ
South Dakota State University
Brookings, SD 57007
Phone: 605-688-5559

KTEQ
Format: eclectic

KTEQ
501 E. St. Joseph
Rapid City, SD 57701
Phone: 605-394-2231

Tennessee

WFSK
Format: eclectic jazz

WFSK
Fisk University
1000-17 Ave. N.
Nashville, TN 37208
Phone: 615-329-8754
Fax: 615-329-8754

WMTS
Format: eclectic

WMTS
P.O. Box 58
Murfreesboro, TN 37132
Phone: 615-898-2636

WRLT
Format: alternative rock

WRLT
401 Church St. #430
Nashville, TN 37219
Phone: 615-242-5600
Fax: 615-242-9877

WRVU
Format: eclectic

WRVU
P.O. Box 9100
Station B
Nashville, TN 37235
Phone: 615-322-3691

Texas

KANM
Format: eclectic

KANM
Texas A&M University
Student Services Bldg.
College Station, TX 77843
Phone: 979-862-2516

KAVC
Format: eclectic

KAVC
P.O. Box 447
Amarillo, TX 79178
Phone: 806-371-5222
Fax: 806-371-5258

KNON
Format: contact program director

KNON
P.O. Box 710909
Dallas, TX 75371
Phone: 214-824-6893

KOOP
Format: eclectic

KOOP
P.O. Box 2116
Austin, TX 78768

Phone: 512-472-1369
Fax: 512-472-6149

KSYM
Format: eclectic

KSYM
1300 San Pedro Ave.
San Antonio, TX 78212
Phone: 210-733-2787
Fax: 210-733-2801

KTRU
Format: eclectic

KTRU
Rice University
P.O. Box 1892
Houston, TX 77005
Phone: 713-348-5878
Fax: 713-348-4893

KTXT
Format: college and alternative

KTXT
Texas Tech University
P.O. Box 43082
Lubbock, TX 79409
Phone: 806-742-3916
Fax: 806-742-3906

KVRX
Format: eclectic

KVRX
P.O. Box D
Austin, TX 78713
Phone: 512-471-5106
Fax: 512-471-8177

Utah

KOHS
Format: alternative rock

KOHS
175 S. 400 E

Orem, UT 84097
Phone: 801-224-9236

KRCL
Format: contact program director

KRCL
1971 West North Temple
Salt Lake City, UT 84116
Phone: 801-363-2801

Vermont

KRUV
Format: eclectic

KRUV
University of Vermont
Burlington, VT 05405
Phone: 802-656-0796

WGDR
Format: eclectic

WGDR
P.O. Box 336
Plainfield, VT 05667
Phone: 802-454-7762

WIUV
Format: contact program director

WIUV
Castleton State College
Castleton, VT 05735
Phone: 802-468-5611

WJSC
Format: contact program director

WJSC
337 College Hill
Johnson, VT 05656
Phone: 802-635-2356

WNUB
Format: contact program director

WNUB
Norwich University
65 South Main St.
Northfield, VT 05663
Phone: 802-485-2435

WRMC

Format: contact program director

WRMC
Middlebury College
Drawer 29
Middlebury, VT 05753
Phone: 802-443-6324

WWLR

Format: contact program director

WWLR
Lyndon State College
Lyndonville, VT 05851
Phone: 802-626-8551

WWPV

Format: eclectic

WWPV
St. Michael's College
P.O. Box 274
Colchester, VT 05439
Phone: 802-654-2334

Virginia

WDCE

Format: eclectic

WDCE
University of Richmond
P.O. Box 85
29 Westhampden Way
Richmond, VA 23173
Phone: 804-289-8698
Fax: 804-289-8996

WEBR

Format: eclectic

WEBR
2929 Eskridge Rd., ste. S
Fairfax, VA 22031
Phone: 703-573-1090

WGMB

Format: contact program director

WGMB
Bridgewater College
402 East College St.
Bridgewater, VA 22812
Phone: 703-828-8501

WLCX

Format: contact program director

WLCX
Longwood College
201 High St.
Farmville, VA 23909
Phone: 804-395-2792

WMWC

Format: contact program director

WMWC
Mary Washington College
1301 College Ave.
Fredericksburg, VA 22401
Phone: 540-654-1710

WODU

Format: eclectic

WODU
Old Dominion
2102 Webb Center
Norfolk, VA 23508
Phone: 757-683-3441
Fax: 757-683-6088

WUVT

Format: eclectic

WUVT
Virginia Tech
350 Squire Student Center

Blacksburg, VA 24061
Phone: 540-231-9880
Fax: 540-231-0150

WVRU
Format: contact program director

WVRU
Radford University
Radford, VA 24142
Phone: 703-831-5020

WXJM
Format: eclectic

WXJM
James Madison University
Anthony Seager Hall
Harrisonburg, VA 22807
Phone: 540-568-6346

Washington

KAGU
Format: contact program director

KAGU
Gonzaga University
E. 502 Boone Ave.
Spokane, WA 99258
Phone: 509-323-3854

KAOS
Format: eclectic

KAOS
Cab 301
Olympia, WA 98505
Phone: 360-867-6893
Fax: 360-867-6797

KCCR
Format: contact program director

KCCR
Pacific Lutheran University
Tacoma, WA 98447
Phone: 206-535-7332

KEZX
Format: eclectic

KEZX
University of Washington
Communications Bldg.
Seattle, WA 98102
Phone: 206-543-3685

KGRG
Format: rock

KGRG
12401 S.E. 320
Auburn, WA 98092
Phone: 253-833-9111, ext.2194
Fax: 253-833-3398

KMIH
Format: Top 40 and dance

KMIH
9100 S.E. Forty-second St.
Mercer Island, WA 98040
Phone: 206-236-3296
Fax: 206-236-3342

KSVR
Format: eclectic

KSVR
2405 E. College Way
Mt. Vernon, WA 98273
Phone: 360-416-7822

KUGS
Format: eclectic

KUGS
Western Washington University
700 Viking Union
Bellingham, WA 98225
Phone: 360-650-2936

KWCW
Format: eclectic

KWCW
Whitman College
345 Boyer Ave.
Walla Walla, WA 99362
Phone: 509-527-5285
Fax: 509-527-4396

KZUU
Format: eclectic

KZUU
Washington State University in
Pullman
Pullman, WA 99164
Phone: 509-335-2208

West Virginia

WSHC
Format: contact program director

WSHC
P.O. Box 3210
Shepherdstown, WV 25443
Phone: 304-846-5134

WWVU
Format: eclectic

West Virginia University
P.O. Box 6446
Mountainliar, WV 26506
Phone: 304-293-3329
Fax: 304-293-7363

Wisconsin

WMSE
Format: eclectic

WMSE
1025 North Broadway
Milwaukee, WI 53202
Phone: 414-277-6942

WMUR
Format: contact program director

WMUR
Marquette University
1131 W. Wisconsin Ave.
421
Milwaukee, WI 53233
Phone: 414-288-1541

WORT
Format: eclectic

WORT
118 S. Bedford St.
Madison, WI 53703
Phone: 608-256-2001
Fax: 608-256-3704

WRFW
Format: eclectic

WRFW
University of Wisconsin—River
Falls
306 North Hall
River Falls, WI 54022
Phone: 715-425-3887

WSUM
Format: contact program director

WSUM
P.O. Box 260020
Madison, WI 53726
Phone: 608-262-1206

WSUW
Format: eclectic

WSUW
University of
Wisconson—Whitewater
1201 Anderson Library
800 Main W.
Whitewater, WI 53190
Phone: 262-472-1323
Fax: 262-472-5029

WWSP
Format: local artists

WWSP
105 CAC
UWSP Reserve St.
Stevens Point, WI 54481
Phone: 715-346-3755
Fax: 715-346-4012

WYRE
Format: eclectic

WYRE
Carroll College
100 N. East Ave.
Waukesah, WI 53186
Phone: 262-521-5201

Wyoming

KZJH
Format: hot adult and classic
rock

KZJH
P.O. Box 2620
Jackson, WY 83001
Phone: 307-733-1770
Fax: 307-733-4760

REFERENCE PUBLICATIONS

**American Society of
Composers, Authors, and
Publishers (ASCAP)**
ASCAP publishes a variety of
manuals and a quarterly
magazine, *Playback,* a
membership publication that
features stories on the industry
and legislative issues. Other
publications include *The ASCAP
License: It Works for You*
(describes copy and performance
rights), *The Essentials of Music
Licensing* (an explanation of how
ASCAP works), *Music for Money*
(discusses the various sources of

publishing and songwriting
income), *Showcases, Workshops
and Grants* (an annual listing of
ASCAP showcases, workshops,
and grants), *What Every Radio
Broadcaster Should Know About
Performances, ASCAP, and
Copyright Law* (a description of
the interaction between radio
stations and ASCAP).

ASCAP Marketing
1 Lincoln Plaza, sixth flr.
New York, NY 10023
Phone: 212-621-6000

ASCAP Licensing Office
2690 Cumberland Parkway, ste.
490
Atlanta, GA 30399
Phone: 800-505-4052

CMJ Directory
A sourcebook which includes
contact information on booking
agents, broadcasters, major and
indie labels, management
companies, indie promotions and
PR firms, music publishers,
retailers, press, and performing
rights societies.

CMJ
810 Seventh Ave., twenty-first flr.
New York, NY 10019
Phone: 646-485-6600
Fax: 646-485-0010

Music Directory Canada
Published every other year, this
directory provides listings for all
aspects of the industry in
Canada.

Music Directory Canada
23 Hanover Dr. #7
St. Catherines, ON L2W 1A3
Canada

Phone: 905-641-1512
Fax: 905-641-1648

Pollstar

Pollstar publishes a variety of
industry directories including a
biannual *Agency Roster,* a
biannual *Record Company
Roster* (executive contacts), a
biannual *Talent Buyer Directory*
(concert promoters and booking
agents for nightclubs, colleges,
and festivals), a biannual *Concert
Venue Directory* (booking and
contact info for arenas and
theaters), an annual *Concert
Support Services Directory*
(contacts for support services
including freight, sound, lighting,
and merchandise), and an
industry-wide phone book called
ConneXion which lists e-mails,
websites, addresses, and fax and
phone numbers. All directories
are free with a subscription to
Pollstar magazine.

Pollstar U.S.A.
4697 W. Jacquelyn Ave.
Fresno, CA 98722
Phone: 559-271-7900
Fax: 559-271-7979

The Music Business Registry

The Music Business Registry
provides a listing of high-level
music industry professionals.

The Music Business Registry, Inc.
7510 Sunset Blvd., ste. 1041
Los Angeles, CA 90046
Phone: 818-769-2722
Fax: 818-769-9808

The Yellow Pages of Rock

The Yellow Pages of Rock
provides a directory of music-
broadcast related individuals and
companies as well as listings of
retailers, major and indie labels,
managers, and booking agents.

The Yellow pages of Rock
120 N. Victory Blvd. third flr.
Burbank, CA 91502
Phone: 800-222-4382
Fax: 818-955-8084

Volunteer Lawyers for the Arts Guide to Copyright for Musicians and Composers

This publication reviews the
various aspects of copyright.

Volunteer Lawyers for the Arts
1 East Fifty-third St.
New York, NY
Phone: 212-319-2787

TRADEMARK INFORMATION AND TRADEMARK SEARCH FIRMS

Thomson & Thomson

A firm that conducts formal
trademark searches.

500 E. St, SW, ste. 940
Washington, D.C. 20024
Phone: 800-356-8630
Web site: www.thomson-
thomson.com

Micropatent

An organization that allows you
to conduct on-line searches of
the U.S. trademark library.

Website: www.micropatent.com

U.S. Trademark Office

Issues trademarks and the forms
necessary to apply for them.
Most forms are available on their
Web site.

U.S. Trademark Office

Assistant Commissioner of
Trademarks
2009 Crystal Drive
Arlington, VA 22202
Website: www.uspto.gov

SAMPLE CLEARANCE COMPANIES

Clearance 13'8"
Phone: 212-580-4654

Diamond Time Ltd.
Phone: 212-274-1938

DMG, Inc.
Phone: 914-248-8319

Sample Clearance Ltd.
Phone: 212-586-2313

Signature Sound, Inc.
Phone: 212-989-0011

MISCELLANEOUS

SeeHear
59 East Seventh St.
New York, NY 10003
Phone: 212-505-9781
Fax: 212-420-7881